STUDIES IN AFRICAN LITERATURE

The Poetry of Okot p'Bitek

Titles from Studies in African Literature published by Heinemann and Africana

A Reader's Guide to African Literature
Hans Zell and Helene Silver

Protest and Conflict in African Literature
Edited by Cosmo Pieterse and Donald Munro

An Introduction to the African Novel
Eustace Palmer

Perspectives on African Literature
Edited by Christopher Heywood

African Writers Talking
Edited by Dennis Duerden and Cosmo Pieterse

The Novels of Chinua Achebe
G. D. Killam

Aspects of South African Literature
Edited by Christopher Heywood

The Poetry of Okot p'Bitek

G. A. HERON
Lecturer in English
Abdullahi Bayero University College
Kano, Nigeria

HEINEMANN
LONDON . IBADAN . NAIROBI . LUSAKA
AFRICANA PUBLISHING COMPANY
NEW YORK

Heinemann Educational Books Ltd
48 Charles Street, London W1X 8AH
P.M.B. 5205, Ibadan . P.O. Box 45314, Nairobi
P.O. Box 3966, Lusaka
EDINBURGH MELBOURNE AUCKLAND TORONTO KINGSTON
HONG KONG SINGAPORE KUALA LUMPUR NEW DELHI

ISBN 0 435 91600 9 (cased)
ISBN 0 435 91601 7 (paper)

First published 1976

Published in the United States of America 1976
by Africana Publishing Company,
a Division of Holmes & Meier Publishers Inc.
101 Fifth Avenue,
New York NY 10003

Library of Congress Card No 76-17068
ISBN 0-8419-0280-1

Printed in Great Britain by
Cox & Wyman Ltd
London, Fakenham and Reading

For Kathleen Casey

CONTENTS

Acknowledgements

THIS book could not have been written without the generous friendship and help of many people who were in Nairobi from 1970 to 1973. I would especially like to thank Angus Calder and Chris Wanjala for their help in launching me on the project, my Acoli teachers, John Odoch and Bob Odoki, for their friendship and the hospitality of their families, and Taban lo Liyong and Okot p'Bitek for the stimulus they gave me and their co-operation in providing essential biographical and background information. I would also like to thank Andy Gurr and Arthur Ravenscroft for their guidance while I was in Leeds, Eric Northey and Ian Munro for their comments on the manuscript, George Vuru for looking over the final versions of my translations from Acoli, and Felix Owolijah for typing the final draft.

G. A. Heron
Kano, December 1975

The author and publisher would like to thank the following:

Okot p'Bitek for permission to reproduce extracts from his B.Litt. thesis (University of Oxford, 1964), *Oral Literature and Its Social Background Among the Acoli and Lang'o*.

East African Publishing House for permission to reproduce extracts from the following publications by Okot p'Bitek: *Song of Lawino; Song of Ocol; Two Songs* and *Wer pa Lawino*.

1 'The Spirit of My Mother'

OKOT P'BITEK professes both a contempt for and an ignorance of the formal study of literature. In a lecture entitled 'What Is Literature?' which he gave at Syracuse University in 1970 he implied that his formal contact with the study of European literature ended abruptly after his School Certificate (A level) examinations:

> When the year ended we made a bonfire of the now useless notebooks and English set books. Somehow I managed to pass the literature paper; but on leaving school, I never read another novel or book of poetry, and never visited the theatre until much later on.
> (Okot p'Bitek, *Africa's Cultural Revolution*, p. 21)

While there is probably a little exaggeration in this boast, since Okot went to a teacher training college immediately after his A levels and thereafter taught English and religious knowledge at a secondary school, the fact that he could make such a claim, or would want to at that point in his career, separates him distinctly from many of his fellows among African writers. It is difficult to imagine Senghor, Soyinka, Okigbo, or, from East Africa, Taban lo Liyong, Ngugi, Kibera, or Ntiru making such a statement; all of these writers have been very much involved in the formal study of a European literary tradition. Okot feels himself fortunate to have undergone little of such study, which he considers inimical to the real purpose of literature:

> Literature is the communication and sharing of deeply felt emotions . . . the aim of any literary activity must be to ensure that there is communication between the singer and the audience, between the story teller and his hearers. . . . This being the case, literature cannot meaningfully be a subject for an examination. Because feeling, not knowledge, is the central aim of any expressive activity. . . . In our schools and universities then literature . . . must be made into a *festival* as it is in the countryside. Let the people sing and dance, let them exchange stories and attend theatres for the joy of it.
> (ibid., pp. 22–3; author's italics)

About the study of the Western literatures which formed the core of the syllabuses in educational systems in most parts of Africa until the mid-1960s at the very earliest, Okot knows relatively little; about literature as a festival of the Acoli countryside he knows a great deal.

The Acoli live in northern Uganda in an area consisting largely of savannah grasslands with a few forested hillsides, stretching northwards from the Murchison area of the Victoria Nile to the Sudanese border. The main administrative centre and the only town of any size in Acoliland is Gulu, which is near the south-west corner of the district. Since 1913 Gulu has been a major mission centre for CMS missionaries (see below p. 106), and Okot's father, Opii Jebedyo, a member of the Pa-Cua clan of the Patiko chiefdom,[1] was one of the many people drawn into Gulu by the missionary activity there. He and his cousin, Festo Okot, left their clan homeland at Ajulu fifteen miles north of Gulu. Festo became a priest and Opii became a teacher.[2] Opii gave up teaching but remained on Church land after a mysterious dream, in which he was told his church would collapse if he ever taught again, came true.[3] Okot's mother, Lacwaa Cerina, came from the Palaro chiefdom, whose homeland is north of Ajulu, and Okot himself was born in Gulu in 1931. He has repeatedly testified to his early interest in oral literature and to his mother's influence in forming that interest:

> ... my interest in African literature ... [was] sparked by my mother's songs and the stories that my father performed around the evening fire.
> (*Africa's Cultural Revolution*, p. 21)

Lacwaa Cerina, like Lawino was 'chief of girls' in her clan in her youth and her interest in music survived the move to Gulu as she continued to be a composer and singer and taught Okot many of the songs he has enjoyed throughout his life and used in many aspects of his varied career. He was closer to his mother than to his father and, despite his travels, her influence continued to be important and he discussed with her everything he did until her death in 1971.

Okot had a prestigious schooling, attending Gulu High School, Kings College Budo, and, from 1952 to 1954, a teacher training course at the Government Training College, Mbarara. Despite the restrictive attitudes then prevalent in mission education, he remained in contact with Acoli music:

> During the school holidays we took part in the 'get stuck' dances although it was strictly prohibited for school children; and during these dances I learnt many songs without any pains, but with great joy and pleasure.
> (*Africa's Cultural Revolution*, p. 21)

Though he was repelled by the examination system and its impositions on school literature he appears to have been a creative student. He wrote and produced an opera in English, called *Acan*, which told the story of a slave boy who wanted to marry a rich girl but could not do so because of their backgrounds, and also a long poem, the manuscript of which he lost, which retold the spear, the bead, and the bean story. (This story is retold in Taban lo Liyong, *Eating Chiefs*, p. 3.) His early literary career was crowned with success with the publication of his Acoli novel *Lak Tar* in 1953 (see below pp. 108–11) and after this he wrote an early version of *Wer pa Lawino* which was rejected by publishers' agents in Gulu in 1956, probably because of its forthrightness on sexual matters. When Okot finished his training, he taught for three years at Sir Samuel Baker's School near Gulu, where he was choirmaster, and while there he married his first wife, Anek. He was a footballer of sufficient skill to be selected for the Uganda national team and he went with them in 1958 on a tour of Britain where he stayed as a student until 1963.

After doing an education diploma at Bristol and a law degree at Aberystwyth, he had the opportunity to pursue his interest in oral literature when he went to Oxford to do a thesis in social anthropology, entitled 'Oral Literature and Its Social Background Among the Acoli and Lang'o'. This involved some field work in Uganda in 1962 and was presented in January 1964. Because of difficulties he encountered during his field work, the bulk of the thesis deals with things Acoli rather than things Lang'o. In relation to the Acoli it contains an introductory chapter on Acoli history and social background and a chapter on Acoli religious ideas, both of which raise many of the controversial issues that figure again in the early chapters of *Religion of the Central Luo*.[4] There is also a section on myths which discusses them in terms of their social function and one on proverbs which arranges them according to the area of social life with which they are concerned (ibid., pp. 38–60 and 317–80). Other types of literary expression discussed are organized according to the occasion of their performance and linked to a description of that occasion (see below pp. 7–10). While work for this thesis involved Okot in further contact with Western scholarship, in relation to the discipline of anthropology, it did not renew his school-time acquaintance with the methods of Western literary criticism. The thesis has very little to say about the literary nature of the songs, and even the vexed question of the literary status of oral works is dealt with in a few lines in the final chapter (ibid., pp. 434–5). The major effect of his studies was to renew and consolidate his contact with oral literature, especially through his field work, at a crucial period of his life. Oral literature has been at the centre of his activities ever since.

On his return to Uganda in 1964, he worked in Gulu for the extra-mural department of Makerere College where, along with other musicians and interested people, he organized the Gulu Festival of Acoli Culture, which was a large and varied event:

> The first year it lasted four days and last year it lasted seven days, and here we have all aspects of culture. We had dances . . . we had an art exhibition, children's play songs, a drama session, and a wonderful session on traditional games. . . .
> (Okot p'Bitek, interview with Robert Serumaga in Dennis Duerden and Cosmo Pieterse (eds), *African Writers Talking*, p. 150)

Okot was both an organizer and a participant, singing and dancing in some of the groups taking part in the festival, which brought together people from all walks of life.[5] Two other important events happened in Gulu at this time. He married his second wife, Auma Kalina Kireng, and he rediscovered, expanded, and translated the poem *Wer pa Lawino* that had been rejected by the publishers in 1956. It was then published, as *Song of Lawino*, in 1966. *Wer pa Lawino* was performed and discussed in and around Gulu, where it attracted a great deal of attention,[6] before the translation was written. Okot says that while working on the Acoli version of the poem he translated a small section of it and read it at a writers' conference in Nairobi and that it was the enthusiastic reception given to this fragment which persuaded him to translate the whole of it. In 1966, Okot was appointed Director of the Uganda Cultural Centre, a centre which, like many in Africa, had previously been dominated by expatriate theatrical groups, though one or two local drama groups were emerging. He transformed the centre, establishing many new activities including a national choir, a puppet theatre, a permanent art exhibition, and regular weekly dance sessions, led by the Heartbeat of Africa troupe.[7] He regarded the centre as a workshop for moulding a national Ugandan culture out of the rich diversity of different local cultures. His activities in the centre culminated in an eight-day festival to coincide with the Independence celebrations in October 1967.

Shortly after this he was dismissed as Director of the Centre whilst on a visit to Zambia during which he made some of the most explicit and extreme criticisms of politicians he has ever made.[8] Since then he has been employed by the University of Nairobi, first at the Adult Studies Centre in Kisumu, where he wrote *Song of Ocol*, 'Song of Prisoner', and 'Song of Malaya', and, since September 1971, at the Institute of African Studies in Nairobi. In both these posts he has continued to organize African cultural events, first through the Kisumu Festival and, from his Nairobi base, through regular cultural festivals throughout the country. He put a brave face on his dismissal from the directorship of the Uganda Cultural Centre, expressing, in an interview with Tony Hall in the *Sunday Nation* (reprinted in *Africa's Cultural Revolution*), casual acceptance of assurances he originally received that this dismissal had nothing to do with what he had written or said:

> The Chairman of the Board of Trustees of the Centre has assured me . . . that whatever I have written or said has not influenced them at all.
> (*Africa's Cultural Revolution*, p. 94.)

It is difficult to believe that he really took his dismissal so lightly; the rest of the interview is full of enthusiasm for what had been started in Kampala. His career in Kenya is a second-best choice. He would naturally prefer to organize cultural festivals in Kampala or Gulu, where he could retain very close links with the Acoli, rather than in Kisumu or Nairobi.

Oral literature shaped Okot's imagination in his infancy and has also been at the centre of his work activities for much of his adult life. I discuss different aspects of the influence of Acoli literature on his poetry in later chapters; the remainder of this chapter introduces the various types of Acoli literature that Okot discusses in his thesis. In her introduction to *Oral Literature in Africa* (p. 2), Ruth Finnegan emphasizes 'the significance of the actual performance . . . of an oral work as the only way . . . in which it can be realized as a literary product'. Many of the comparisons I make between oral and written literature isolate the verbal element of the oral work in much the way Ruth Finnegan warns against (ibid., pp. 3–4)[9] and therefore tend implicitly to underestimate that work. Finnegan also points out 'the significance of the actual occasion' for which an oral work is composed. This, she says, 'can directly affect the detailed content and form of the work being performed':

> Oral pieces are not composed in the study and later transmitted through the impersonal and detached medium of print, but tend to be directly involved in the occasions of their utterance. Some of the poetry . . . is specifically 'occasional', in that it is designed for and arises from particular situations like funerals, weddings, celebrations of victory, soothing a baby, accompanying work, and so on; again, with certain prose forms (like, for instance, proverbs), appropriateness to the occasion may be more highly valued by local critics than the verbal content itself. But even when there is not this specific connection, a piece of oral literature tends to be affected by such factors as the general purpose and atmosphere of the gathering at which it is rendered, recent events in the minds of performer and audience, or even the time of year and propinquity of the harvest.
> (ibid., pp. 11–12)

I briefly describe the occasion of performance of each type of literature discussed to provide a background for the comparisons in later chapters.

Okot's thesis describes in detail the occasion of performance of all the types of literature he discusses except myths and proverbs. In his chapter on myths, there is only a vague hint of the occasion of their telling, when he describes the myth of his own clan, the Pa-Cua (see below p. 88). He writes that he was told the myth when his father gave him a bow and some arrows, adding that girls who marry into the clan are also told it shortly after their marriage ('Oral Literature Among the Acoli and Lang'o', pp. 61 and 65). This would seem to confirm Ruth Finnegan's treatment of myths as a specialized kind of prose narrative (*Oral Literature in Africa*, p. 361). For most African oral literatures no prosodic system has yet been isolated.[10] Okot suggests that the defining factor could be that verse is sung and prose is spoken, leaving folk stories, myths, and proverbs as prose forms and chants at the ancestral shrine and the songs sung at various dances as poetry ('Oral Literature Among the Acoli and Lang'o', pp. 434–5). Myths and folk tales are therefore the only narrative forms in Acoli oral literature.

Stories are told in the informal situation of a family gathering immediately before and after the evening meal. While the women are still cooking, the story telling begins:

> The first stories are simple and short and are directed towards the younger members of the family.
>
> '*Ododo-na in yo*' someone calls out. Anyone may volunteer to begin. 'My story, listen.' As soon as the story teller has come to the end of his story, he chooses the next person to perform, and this could be anyone present.
> (ibid., pp. 387–9)

The bringing of the meal and the separation of men and women into two groups to eat interrupts the story telling, but after the meal the women join the men and the tales resume. Now, as the children begin to fall asleep, the stories become 'longer and more profound. They treat the problems arising from the relations between youths *inter se* and between youths and adults' (ibid., p. 390). Often young people are tempted away from the family group by dances near by and then the stories change character again:

> The man and his wives, and any adult visitors, now exchange witty folk tales dealing with the problems of the grown-ups. . . . [These tales] are directed against particular individuals or groups. They are meant to expose certain undesirable traits in the character of one or more of, or of someone connected with, the listeners.
> (ibid., pp. 392–4)

All three groups of tales use the same conventions, representing human life in the behaviour of stock animal characters like Hare and Hyena, or semi-human characters like the dwarf, Lagitin (ibid., pp. 398–401), and from synopses the three groups might be indistinguishable from each other. Yet in their telling the expectations of the listeners would be very different and the kinds of detail and modes of dramatization used by the teller would also be different.

In contrast, the most formal situation in which singing is used within a clan community is during the dedication of an ancestral shrine which occurs some time after the death of an old man of the lineage. The dead man is said to call for the building of the shrine through the dreams of the living head of the clan and all adult members of the clan are invited to the homestead where it is to be built. A joint council of the living and the dead is held inside a hut to discuss various issues relating to the welfare of the clan; the dead speak through a medium. Then the goats and chickens brought for the ancestors are offered and beer and cooked meat left on the new shrine. After that, the whole clan gathers and chants its requests for help from the ancestors, led by the son of the dead man whose shrine has been built:

Leader: *Wan tin watedo wora*
Tin wamiyo ire remo
Wamiye gweno ki kongo
Kom dano obed ma yot
People: *Kom dano obed ma yot*
Leader: *Ngu otoo*
People: *Otoo, otoo, otoo*
Leader: *Tong obed ma bit*
People: *Obed ma bit, bit, bit*
etc.

Leader: Today we have cooked [a feast for]
my father
Today we have given him blood
We have given him chicken and beer
Let the people have good health
People: Let the people have good health
Leader: Lions let them die
People: Let them die, die, die
Leader: The spears let them be sharp
People: Let them be sharp, sharp, sharp
etc.
(*Religion of the Central Luo*, pp. 94–9)

A less formal event within a homestead is the spirit possession dance. This is a part of the means used to deal with 'ill-health or other misfortune' considered to be 'due to certain spirits' (ibid., pp. 106–9). Once the diviner has established the spirit involved, he sings its own 'praise songs' to it whilst offering it gifts, as in this song to Jok Kulu (River Jok) which was often considered responsible for 'Miscarriage and other illness connected with pregnancy':

Twon-gweno pa Kulu en
Eiya, Eiya,
Kic bene mitte me ananga
Eiya, Eiya,
Labolo mitte me amwonya
Eiya, Eiya

A cock for Kulu is here
Oh yes, Oh yes,
Honey is also wanted for eating
Oh yes, Oh yes,
Banana is wanted for eating
Oh yes, Oh yes.
(ibid., pp. 108–9)

Both these kinds of verse are only meaningful within their immediate context in the life of the community.

Bwola and *otole* dance songs were sung during elaborate and expensive political occasions which involved the whole of a chiefdom. With the decline of the institution of the traditional chiefdom in this century (see below, pp. 105–6), they have almost died out, except as museum pieces for performance in front of the President or visiting dignitaries (*Africa's Cultural Revolution*, p. 30). The *bwala* dance was performed in the chief's enclosure on important occasions like coronations and the songs associated with it celebrated the power of the chief and his lineage ('Oral Literature Among the Acoli and Lang'o', p. 82). The *otole* dance cemented the relationship between friendly chiefdoms by the mock invasion of one chiefdom by members of another. It began with an attack in war formation from outside the village by the visitors, during which there might be considerable destruction of crops and cattle, and then led to a competition inside the village dancing arena, the various groups seeking to dominate the dancing with their own songs. *Otole* dance steps represent the formations and movements of battle and each chiefdom had its own repertoire of songs which celebrated the exploits in war of its own chiefdom and was deliberately provocative to others (ibid., pp. 75–80; see below, pp.85–7).

Funeral songs are sung at the *guru lyel* ceremony which usually takes place in the dead person's homestead some months after his death and marks the end of the period of mourning. As each group of relatives arrives, they pretend to be warriors storming the homestead whilst singing a song of the attack on death, like this one:

Soloist: *Yee, mac owang Layima ye,*
Mac owang kulu Cumu.

Chorus: *Owang nginyinginyi woko;*
Kono ao pa min to:
Soloist: *Nyara kono ariyo raa ma bor;*
Chorus: *Kono ao pa min to,*
Kono awango nginyinginyi woko;
Mac owang kulu Cumu ye!

Soloist: Oh, fire rages at Layima, oh,
Fire rages in the valley of river Cumu.
Chorus: Everything is utterly utterly destroyed;
If I could reach the homestead of death's mother:
Soloist: My daughter, I would make a long grass torch,
Chorus: If I could reach the homestead of death's mother,
I would destroy everything utterly utterly;
Like the fire that rages in the
valley of river Cumu oh!
(Okot p'Bitek, *Horn of My Love*, p. 126)

Later in the day, these songs are replaced by songs of surrender to death and acceptance of its finality and eventually they become more concerned with the living. The end of the period of mourning is the occasion of the beginning of competition for the man's inheritance and the wife who is left behind has considerable choice in the matter of who should inherit her. By the end of the funeral the problems of inheritance are uppermost in people's minds ('Oral Literature Among the Acoli and Lang 'o', pp. 197–207); see below, pp. 84–5).

The *orak* or *larakaraka* dance,[11] is the least formal and therefore the most common of Acoli dances because it is attached to no single occasion and 'to hold it no chief's authority or permission is required'. ('Oral Literature Among the Acoli and Lang'o', p. 293). It is held in connection with a marriage, at the end of *otole* dances and after *awak* communal work parties. It is a fairly local activity, primarily for the unmarried young men and women of a group of clans 'living within a few hours' walk' (ibid., p. 298) of each other. Most *orak* songs have a short life:

> Unlike the *otole* and *bwala* songs, and also to some extent the funeral dirges, the *orak* songs are very transitory. . . . The vast majority of them treat local issues; and the jokes, the 'twist of the tail', are understood only locally. (ibid., pp. 303–4)

The singer-composers of the songs enjoy no special economic status but are widely known and well-respected in their area. Songs on certain subjects, for example the reputation of soldiers during the Second World War for sexual misconduct (see below, pp. 142–5), may spread over a wide area. Radio has made certain singers, like the blind singer from Lamogi, Omal Adok Too (mentioned in Okot p'Bitek, *Song of Ocol*, p. 34),[12] popular throughout Acoliland, though they are not full-time performers. Songs are commonly used to illustrate crucial parts of stories told around the evening fire and the singing often involves the hearers as well as the teller. In one children's tale the semi-human ogre Obibi visits the homestead while only children are there and tries to persuade them to leave with him. He involves them in a mock tug-of-war, one end of the rope tied round his testicles and the children pulling at the other, and the children and the story teller sing this song:

> Children: *Ngat muweko ywayo likwayo oloye*
> Obibi: *Uru-uc likwaya ywaya mot mot*
>
> Children: Who so fails to pull his grandchildren
> Obibi: (cry of pain) My grandchildren pull me gently, gently.
> ('Oral Literature Among the Acoli and Lang'o', pp. 387–8)

The more informal kinds of song can be sung by people casually, outside the occasions of the dances. Some married men have a *nanga*, the small harp used by great musicians:

> Acoli men live playing this harp. They play it to themselves, brooding, thinking of a girl. They play it while strolling about, in company round the evening fire, and to entertain guests.
> (Cliff Lubwa p'Chong, 'Vernacular Themes in Our Schools')

Women also sing to themselves while they are working during the day, as Lawino tells us she used to do while working at the grinding stone with her sister (p. 74).[13]

When written literature is introduced into this situation where literary expression is usually linked to the immediate concerns of a fairly small community it is inevitably alien in some respects, however much of its technique or content it borrows from the oral literature of the community. A distinction between the writer and the performer is inherent in the use of a written text. *Wer pa Lawino* and *Song of Lawino* are both performable and have been performed. The Acoli version particularly was performed many times before its publication and may have reached a fair proportion of its audience through oral performance rather than silent reading. But the performer of either poem has had his creative role shorn from him because the fixed nature of the written text severely limits his ability to relate the performance to the immediate concerns of his hearers. The verbal element of the performance is elevated to a position of predominance over dramatic and musical elements which it does not necessarily hold in oral literature. There are therefore many dangers involved in the comparisons made in the following chapter between Okot's poems and the written versions which isolate the verbal elements of oral songs. It is important to be continuously aware of the partial picture of an oral song that a written version gives.

Notes to Chapter 1

1. For more information on the chiefdom system, see below, pp. 103–4 and 106.
2. Okot p'Bitek, *Religion of the Central Luo*, p. 88.
3. Conversation with Okot p'Bitek, as with other biographical information not otherwise referenced.
4. Okot p'Bitek, 'Oral Literature and its Social Background Among the Acoli and Lang'o', pp. 1–33 and 179–91; c.f. *Religion of the Central Luo*, pp. 10–56.
5. *Africa's Cultural Revolution*, p. 22.
6. *Ibid.*, p. 44.
7. *Ibid.*, pp. 95–6.
8. *Ibid.*, pp. 6–14.
9. Unfortunately it is precisely this aspect [the importance of performance] which is most often overlooked in recording and interpreting instances of oral literature. This is . . . due . . . to the unconscious reference constantly made by both recorders and readers to more familiar written forms. This model leads us to think of the *written* element as the primary and thus somehow the most fundamental material in every kind of literature—a concentration on the *words* to the exclusion of the vital and essential aspect of performance. It cannot be too often emphasized that this insidious model is a profoundly misleading one in case of oral literature.' (Author's italics.)
10. See Joseph Greenberg, 'A Survey of African Prosodic Systems' in Stanley Diamond (ed.) *Culture in History*, p. 928.
11. Described twice by Lawino, the second time as the 'get-stuck' dance (*moko*) when it is performed by moonlight, see *Song of Lawino* (Nairobi: East African Publishing House, 1966), pp. 31–5 and 118. All further page references to *Song of Lawino* are to the same edition.
12. Mentioned in Okot p'Bitek, *Song of Ocol* (Nairobi: East African Publishing House, 1970), p. 34. All further page references to *Song of Ocol* are to the same edition.
13. This account of Acoli oral literature refers to all the types of song discussed fully in Okot's thesis. This is not comprehensive, as the women's *ogodo* dance, for example, is not discussed, but it is sufficient to provide examples for comparison and to justify the generalizations made.

2 The Rhetoric of the Poems

FORMALLY *Song of Ocol* and 'Song of Malaya' are a collection of monologues addressed to a number of different individuals or social groups. *Song of Lawino* and 'Song of Prisoner' are each a single monologue, the one predominantly addressed to Ocol and the other to the courtroom where the prisoner first heard the question that now repeatedly recurs in his mind:

Do you plead
Guilty
Or
Not guilty?[1]

In all cases the people addressed are invoked by their names or by titles, as in these lines from *Song of Lawino*:

Ocol, jal, in iloko akakaa
In yang' inena ma a-pudi[2]

Ocol, my husband,
My friend,
What are you talking?
You saw me when I was young. (p. 44)

The words '*Ocol, jal*' in the Acoli and 'Ocol, my husband / My friend' in the translation are examples of the rhetorical device of apostrophe. Apostrophe is used in Okot's poems to introduce the dramatic confrontations which cause each singer's outbursts. Its use intensifies the emotions in particular passages and the choice of respectful or disrespectful titles contributes to the different tones of the poems. Okot's extensive use of this device reflects its use in Acoli oral songs, where it performs many of the same functions. By borrowing this technique, Okot creates an illusion that he has retained the relationship between singer and audience which arises from the conditions of performance of oral literature, though the audience addressed in his 'Songs' is a fictional one. It also provides a framework for the loquacious and discursive manner that gives his poetry so distinctive a flavour when contrasted with the compressed and compact style of Soyinka, Okigbo, or Ntiru.

Apostrophe dramatizes the idea of 'communication between the singer and the audience' that Okot sees as 'the aim of any literary activity'. The people who are addressed may be observers of, or participants in, the events that lie behind the song. Where the second person ('you') is used together with apostrophe, the people addressed usually have a role in the situation from which the song arises; where the song is in the third person throughout, they are likely to represent a supposed audience being asked to share in the attitudes or emotions of the singer. Apostrophe of the second kind occurs very often in Acoli funeral songs, where the bereaved call on other members of the family to share in their grief:

Anyongo wi yat
Calo winyo;
An calo ayom
Munyongo wi yat.
Ai, maa,
Wi-lobo ogungu koma;
An awac ango?
Ee, wi-lobo gungu koma;
Can omoto i koma, ee!

I am squatting on a tree
Like a bird;
I am like a monkey
Squatting on a tree.
Oh, mother,
Fate has knelt on me;
What can I say?
Ee, fate has crushed me completely;
Suffering has sunk deeply in my flesh, ee!
(*Horn of My Love*, p. 132)

One of the occasions when Lawino uses apostrophe in this way is in the ironic context of her 'bereavement' at the 'death' of Ocol. Section 12 of her 'Song' begins with an appeal to the clansmen to share her grief:

Winy lu-tua an akoko cwara
Ma wiye olal woko i tim, (p. 135)

Listen my clansmen
I cry over my husband
Whose head is lost (p. 199)

At the end of the same section she calls on them again to 'cry together' with her to 'mourn the death of my husband' (p. 207).

The appeals to those other than Ocol in the early sections of the poem similarly involve them only minimally in her situation. They are being asked only to listen: '*Lutuwa an akok, winyu dwona*' (p. 12), 'My clansmen, I cry / Listen to my voice' (p. 15), but in these sections the emotion she wishes them to share is not one of sorrow, but usually of bemused wonderment at the goings-on of Ocol, Clementine, and their friends, particularly the women:

Lutua pooro tino pa mon onyo! (p. 21)

O! my clansmen
How aged modern women
Pretend to be young girls! (p. 25)

Ocol's appeal to 'Mother, mother,' at the end of Section 2 of his poem is similar in that it is in the context of Ocol's deepest expression of sorrow, in his case sorrow that he 'was . . . born / Black' (p. 22) and doesn't involve the person addressed in the situation beyond its appeal for sympathy. There appears to be a slight increase in the involvement of the fictional audience in this next song in that the singer asks 'Abong' to act:

Oteka lwenyo kene,
Twon kara to kene ada!
Abong kony omeru ba;
En acel to woko do!
Obalo ngo pa jo pa Awic?
Omera lwenyo kene?

The warrior fights alone
Behold the bull dies alone, oh!
Abong, why, help your brother;
The only one, he is dying, oh!
What wrong has he done to the children of Awic?
Why should my brother fight death alone?
(*Horn of My Love*, p. 123)

This is an appeal for impossible action. Its taunting cruelty in suggesting that Abong is doing less than his duty by his brother underlines the loneliness of death which is the main emotion of the song. Lawino's one appeal for advice from the clansmen is similar in its effects:

> My clansmen, I ask you:
> What has become of my husband?
> Is he suffering from boils?
> Is it ripe now?
> Should they open it
> So that the pus may flow out? (p. 46)

The clansmen are really being asked to laugh with Lawino at Ocol, not to give advice. This appeal is not radically different from the other appeals to the clansmen; they are observers, not participants in the poem.

Many Acoli oral songs use the second person to refer to those whom the singer addresses. One way of dealing with the historical events in *otole* or *bwola* songs is to dramatize them, with the singer assuming the voice of an observer of the situation and addressing himself to the historical participants. Similarly, at the *orak* dance, the singer occasionally sings *to* his victim, rather than about him. The singers at the ancestral shrine sing to the ancestors, and the spirit possession songs are often addressed to the '*jok*', the spirit who has caused the trouble, as in this song to Jok Kulu:

> *Twon gweno pud okok ku*
> *Kulu dok tu*
> *Kulu wangi oto?*
> *Dok tu.*

> The cock has not yet crowed
> [It is not yet too late]
> Kulu go back to your home
> Kulu, are your eyes dead?
> Go back to your home.
> (*Religion of the Central Luo*, p. 110)

Funeral songs are often to the dead person, or, near the end of the funeral, to the inheritor. The whole of 'Song of Malaya', most of *Song of Ocol* and over half of *Song of Lawino* and 'Song of Prisoner' are written in the second person.

Some oral songs contain a change from the use of third person to the use of second person in the course of the song as in this example from the first stanza of the song '*Nya pa Lekamoi*':

Ai maa,
Ineno nya pa Lekamoi
Mudongo nyen.
Nyako dwogo awene ka?
Meya bino awene?
Nya pa twon,
Dako bi aneni, nye;
Nya pa Lekamoi,
Lawi anyira . . .

Oh, mother,
Behold the daughter of Lekamoi
Who has just grown up.
Young woman, when will she return?
When does my love come back?
Daughter of the bull,
Woman, come, let me see you, listen;
Daughter of Lekamoi,
Leader of the girls . . .
(*Horn of My Love*, p. 43)

At the beginning of the song, the singer refers to his love in the third person and uses apostrophe to address '*Maa*' in much the way we have already discussed, but later in the stanza he talks to the girl he loves using the second person. When he switches from speaking to an observer to speaking to a participant the appeal in his use of apostrophe changes from an appeal for sympathy to an appeal for help. The use of apostrophe to the lover is necessary to indicate who is being addressed as 'you' and the change to the second person helps to build up to a climax. The use of apostrophe to Ocol, combined with the change to the second person at the end of Sections 2 and 6 in *Song of Lawino*, is similar in that it implies a demand for Ocol to do something and summarizes sections that are predominantly in the third person. Section 2 ends with Lawino trying to reason with Ocol: '*Wek cac liwota, wek cac, / Kit Acol tye ma beco,*' (p. 25). 'Listen Ocol, my old friend, / The ways of your ancestors / Are good,' (p. 29). In Section 6, she ends her comparison of Acoli and European cooking with an appeal for '. . . freedom / To eat what one likes' (p. 80).[3] The whole poem has a similar climax in the use of the second person in Sections 13 and (in Acoli) 14, where Lawino seeks to an end the bickering in the early sections and restore Ocol to health and normality.

In the second stanza of the funeral song '*Liwota ling doga*' (My beloved speaks not to me) the use of the second person introduces nostalgia about the relationship of the singer to his dead lover:

Larema lok kweda ba!
Omera ka ito
Pwoyo luykwa weng
Can dyang ki remo ye!
Lamo tino ye!

My friend speak to me please!
My brother if you be dead
Let them bury both of us
Lack of cattle and friendship, oh!
My lover since [days of] youth oh!
('Oral Literature Among the Acoli and Lang'o', p. 213)

The change to the second person at the beginning of Sections 3, 4 and 5 of *Song of Lawino* provides a similar nostalgic reminder of the past relationship of Lawino and Ocol to explain the background to the arguments that follow. The nostalgia is most extended in Section 4. Lawino begins by remembering her own beauty when she was younger, then describes Ocol's wooing of her, referring to him in the third person, and finally confronts him in the second person, reminding him of the things he used to admire in her:

Komi yang' myel pi kedo kora, (p. 38)

You trembled
When you saw the tattoos
On my breasts (p. 45)

In the song '*Ceng ma too peke*', 'If death were not there', the switch to the second person has a more aggressive purpose. The whole song is an elaboration of the question with which it begins:

Ceng ma too peke,
La-laku lako gin ango?

If death were not there
Where would the inheritor get things?
(*Horn of My Love*, p. 143)

For the first nine lines the question is addressed to no one in particular, but in the middle of the song the singer confronts the inheritor himself, who will almost certainly be present when the song is sung, though the singer may still be guessing exactly who it is going to be:

Nye, omera, in mono,
Ceng ma too peke,
La-rac, inyomo nya pa anga?
Dako odong ki la-laku do;
Ee, la-laku kwo kanye?
Oto odong ki la-laku do . . .

Ee, brother, tell me,
If death were not there,
Ugly man, whose daughter would have married you?
A wife has been left for the inheritor;
Ee, inheritor, how would you have lived?
The house has been left for the inheritor . . .
(loc. cit.)

The song ends with a repetition of the question that began it, again referring to the inheritor in the third person, but the direct question to the inheritor increases the impact of the mockery throughout the song. At the end of Section 4 of her 'Song', Lawino mocks Ocol for his ignorance of Acoli games, songs, and dances by direct questions, for example '*Wer bwola adii ma igoyo?*' (p. 41),[4] 'And you cannot sing one song' (p. 48). In Section 12 the summary of Lawino's contempt for Ocol, in which she calls him first a 'dog' and then a 'woman', interrupts the lament at his 'death' directed to the clansmen (see above, p. 13) with a switch to the use of the second person (*Wer pa Lawino*, pp. 140–1; *Song of Lawino*, pp. 204–7).

By the manner in which he addresses someone, the kind of names or titles he uses to refer to a person, a singer can use apostrophe to contribute to the tone of a song. The song '*Nya pa Lekamoi*' (see above, p. 16) uses four praise names for the girl the singer loves, as well as her personal name ('Abul'). In the funeral song '*Woko okelo ayela*' (Fate has brought troubles) the singer uses oblique, respectful titles to describe his relationship with his brother, calling him first '*Gin pa maa, / Wod pa Labwor*', 'Beloved of my mother / Son of Labwor', and later '*Latin pa abaa, / Nyodo pa Labwor*', 'Child of my father / Son of Labwor' (*Horn of My Love*, p. 133). Lawino frequently uses two or three names for Ocol together to him, as in the line: '*Cwara, Ocol, jal, nenni lit!*' (p. 22).[5] (My husband, Ocol, friend, you are sick!) In the first twenty-four lines of the Acoli version, translated by the first thirty-three lines in the English version, she appeals to Ocol as '*cwara*', 'husband', '*la-coo*' (man), '*Wod-wegi*', 'Son of the Chief', '*Larema, la-lwak omera*', 'my friend, age-mate of my brother', '*jal*', 'friend' and finally 'Ocol' (*Wer pa Lawino*, pp. 11–12; *Song of Lawino*, pp. 13–14).[6] At the end of the poem, in Section 13, she appeals to him as '*wod twon*', 'son of the bull', and '*Rwot*',[7] 'Son of the Chief' (*Wer pa*

Lawino, pp. 144 and 146; *Song of Lawino*, pp. 212 and 216), and the last paragraph in the English version names him in four ways:

> Let me dance before you,
> My love
> Let me show you
> The wealth in your house,
> Ocol my husband,
> Son of the Bull,
> Let no one uproot the Pumpkin. (p. 216)[8]

In contrast, the other singers refer to people in the most abrupt, direct way possible: for Ocol, Lawino is simply 'Woman' (p. 9), for the Prisoner, his father is 'My old man' (p. 36), and the commonest way of invoking others is by using the word 'You . . .', as in 'You Karamojong elder . . .' (*Song of Ocol*, p. 45), 'You vigorous young sailor . . .' (*Two Songs*, p. 127), or 'You pressmen of the World . . .' (ibid., p. 90). Lawino's use of oblique respectful titles reflects the fact that she is the only one of the singers living within a peasant community in which the titles and praise names are still meaningful and also helps to create a difference in tone between the aggression of the other singers and the more dignified, persuasive tone of Lawino. At the beginning and the end of the poem particularly, Lawino stresses everything that binds her to Ocol and leads her to expect from him a certain kind of behaviour.

In certain songs the apostrophe used is essential to the structure of the song because it is the main indicator of the situation that the singer is singing about. Below is an *orak* song in which a composer with a considerable reputation comments indirectly on his ability to 'kill' his enemies by the effect his mockery has on their reputations. It is in the form of a dialogue between 'Lagama', the man who was 'killed', and a 'bystander':

> *Lagama, icito kanyi?*
> *Acito tung pa too.*
> *Cimot too*
> *Iyo, iyo.*
> *Lapailyec owero wer*
> *Wer neko Okoli*
> *Iyo, iyo, Ndio*
> *Apwoyo motti*
> *Dong koni aci moto!*

> Lagama, where are you going to?
> I am going to the homestead of death.
> (I am dead.)

Take my greetings to death [if you are really dead]
  Certainly, certainly.
The man from Pailyec [the singer] has composed a song
The song has killed Okoli.
  Certainly, certainly, yes
  Thanks for the good wishes
  In a few moments I will greet 'death'.
('Oral Literature Among the Acoli and Lang'o', p. 291)

The singer creates the idea of the dialogue and of the participants within it in the minimum of space by the use of apostrophe in the first line. In a similar way, the apostrophe at the beginning of *Song of Lawino* combined with Lawino's reports of Ocol's complaints against her enables Lawino to show us the main outlines of her predicament and the nature of her dispute with Ocol much more economically than she could with a narrative form. By the end of those first thirty-three lines we know of the marriage relationship between Ocol and Lawino, that they are now involved in a serious dispute, and we know the basis of Ocol's reason for attacking Lawino, as well as the kind of counterattack she is making. Our understanding of what is going on in the rest of the poem depends on this extremely brief introduction.

Lawino keeps this situation constantly in the reader's mind and makes the poem almost into a dialogue, with one side of the argument very distorted, by regularly reporting Ocol's words. The second half of the first stanza, addressed to the clansmen and referring to Ocol in the third person, clarifies the initial introduction of the situation a little by summarizing all Ocol's concerns. She begins with his attack on her herself:

Yeta ki dum Munu, loko ki awaka,
Ni an mucanyi, en pe emita: (p. 12)

He abuses me in English
And he is so arrogant.
He says I am rubbish,
He no longer wants me! (p. 15)

Then she tells us of his abuse of her clansmen:

Yeto maro-ni la-tyet
Ni paneya ming' . . . (p. 13)

He says my mother is a witch
That my clansmen are fools (p. 16)

Finally she reports his contempt for all black men:

> *Ni kit Acol racu atika-tika,*
> *Ni Acol pud gudong' ang'ec* (p. 13)
>
> He says Black People are primitive
> And their ways are utterly harmful (p. 17)

Passages of a couple of paragraphs or more beginning with 'Ocol says' or 'he says' occur in most sections of the poem. These passages relate the section to Lawino's dispute with Ocol and provide Lawino with her subject matter when she launches into her longer and better argued replies.

The immediate physical position of the singer in 'Song of Prisoner' is explained to us by his description, but the essential confrontation between him and the warders and the remembered figure of the judge is made clear again by apostrophe. The prisoner asks the warder when he speaks to him as 'Brother' in Section 1 how he can beat such a weak man and asks the judge a few lines later why he is being punished before being found guilty (pp. 15–16). These two questions explain the dramatic situation behind the poem. We are reminded of the situation by the prisoner's repeated attempts to enter a plea in answer to the judge's courtroom question (*Two Songs*, pp. 12, 30, 32, and 44–5). The question itself appears four times in the poem and is brought into the reader's mind in many other places when the prisoner attempts to answer it. In Section 2 for example, he pleads 'hunger' (p. 23) and in Section 13 he pleads guilty to 'pride' (p. 100). In this way his confrontation with warders and judge is kept in mind for the whole of the poem.

In the dialogue oral song '*Kel kweyo*' (Bring sand), apostrophe is equally vital to the structure of the song but it is used in a more complex way to involve five characters in the story. It tells of a girl who is being encouraged by her mother and father to marry an old man and is at the same time being wooed by a young man. Only two of the characters, the young man and the girl sing, but the words and actions of the others are implicit in the ways in which they are addressed by the two singers. The young man sings to the girl, Acli, asking her to give him a token of her love by bringing him some of the fine sand used by the Acoli for polishing their teeth. Instead of replying, the girl sings to her mother, and we learn of the pressure that is on her to marry the old man:

> *Nyako: Ee, akwero kwe do maa,*
> *Maa, wek reere, do maa?*
>
> Girl: Ee, but I have rejected the man, mother
> Mother, but why are you so stubborn?
> (*Horn of My Love*, pp. 54–6)

Later we learn from the young man that the old man is actually on the scene:

> *Laco:* *Ee, Acii meya,*
> *Laracci ogudu bad meya?*
> *Ee, laditti nye,*
> *Cit cen, nye . . .*
>
> Man: Ee, Acii my love,
> The ugly man, has he touched the arm of my beloved?
> Ee, old man, listen,
> Go away, do you hear?
> (loc. cit.)

In the girl's next stanza we learn that her father is also encouraging the old man:

> *Nyako:* *Ai, ai, an do wora*
> *Wora, an akwero kwe do wora;*
> *Ai, ai an adeg gira . . .*
>
> Girl: Oh, oh, me, oh father
> Father, but I have rejected the man, oh father;
> Oh, oh, I do not want the man . . .
> (loc. cit.)

The young man repeats his call to Acii to 'bring sand' and Acii tries 'in vain' to get away to him:

> *Nyako:* *Laditti, nye,*
> *Wek kong atwe yen ki maa;*
> *Ai, ai, acona ni, nye,*
> *Wek kong anyar raa ki maa,*
> *Ee, okunga ni, nye,*
> *Kur kong aom pii ki maa.*
> *Wora, an akwora kwe do, wora;*
> *Won lim gire obilo abaa!*
>
> Girl: You old thing, listen,
> Wait, let me first collect firewood for my mother;
> You ugly one, listen, oh,

Wait, let me first bring cooking grass for my mother;
Oh, oh, the ugly man, oh father,
Let me fetch some water for my mother.
Father, but I have rejected the old man, father;
The wealthy man has bewitched my father.
(loc. cit.)

All of the action of this little drama is implicit in the apostrophe that is used in it.

In *Song of Ocol* and 'Song of Malaya' confrontations between the singer and a number of different individuals are shown to the reader through the apostrophe used. The single word 'Woman' (p. 9) that begins *Song of Ocol* is intended to remind the reader of Lawino's 'Song' which is the subject matter of Section 1. Lawino's 'tears' (p. 75) relate Section 8 to the same dispute. Elsewhere Ocol reports the words of those he addresses to provide him with an opportunity to express his own ideas. In this way he picks up the supposed whispering of 'My friend and Comrade':

Do I hear you whisper
  Who is that man?
  What is his name?
Do you not know me
And my brothers-in-power? (p. 55)

The malaya also briefly reports the attitudes and actions of many of those she addresses before she begins her counterattack on them; thus it is the reported jealousy of her 'married sister' (p. 147) that preludes her explanation of her contribution to family life in returning the husband '. . . smiling / Like a boy of fifteen' (p. 148). In these sections these poems become dialogues with one side of the argument ill-represented and distorted in the same way as in Lawino's 'dialogue' with Ocol. There is no other confrontation in 'Song of Prisoner' except that between him and the judge and warders. His use of apostrophe to people other than them adds to our knowledge about him, the sections to his mother, father, and wife confirming the poverty of his background and the section to the widow indicating the assassin prisoner's attitude to the assassination.

Some sections of *Song of Ocol* and 'Song of Malaya' involve attacks on groups of people rather than individuals and in these the apostrophe, instead of merely introducing the conflict in the section, tends to spread and occupy considerable space. The malaya's attack on her occupational hazard, venereal disease, is in the form of mockery of two of its victims, the 'Big Chief' and the 'Bwana', together with a request to influential people from schoolteachers to presidents to do something more towards the eradication of '. . . . this one pest' (p. 140). Ocol's commentary on the role of women in traditional African societies uses three descriptions of overburdened women in undignified situations. We see them carrying a pot of water on the head and a sack on the back and being encouraged to grow fat by their mothers because fatness is considered attractive. Then Ocol commands them to break out of the situation before his final dismissal of a woman's traditional role:

Woman of Africa
Whatever you call yourself,
Whatever the bush poets
Call you
You are not
A wife! (p. 43)

About half of Ocol's mockery of the role of pastoral groups is in the form of apostrophe to them, combined with a very short description of their activities, varying from two lines for the Jie to the seventy-two-line history and commentary on the Kalenjin. All of this leads to the pivotal word 'Listen' (p. 49) which is followed in the second half of the section by Ocol's declaration of his violent intention for the future of people like them.

The same technique is used in Section 1 of 'Song of Malaya'; the malaya indicates the range of her clientele and thus her social importance by welcoming all her visitors from all sections of society into her home. The apostrophe to these customers combined with short descriptions or comments on them takes up all except the last seventeen lines of the section (pp. 127–35). There is even less description in *Song of Ocol* when Ocol uses the titles of all the dignitaries of the new African states whom he addresses to illustrate the residual colonial influence he is mocking:

Your Excellency
Bwana President
I salute you,
And you Honourable Ministers
Discussing the White Paper;
Mister Speaker, Sir,
You Backbenchers
And Opposition chiefs,
Greetings to you! (p. 81)

He only needs to add a short request to the end of the long collection of English names of officials throughout the society:

Talk about
The African foundation
On which we are
Building the new nations
Of Africa (p. 83)

The titles tell their own story; apostrophe has almost become an independent form of poetry.

The rhetoric of apostrophe is the only major formal influence of oral literature on Okot's practice as a writer of poetry which has survived translation. A few other features of oral songs which had a marked effect on *Wer pa Lawino* have had a reduced effect on *Song of Lawino* or have disappeared because Okot concentrated on an extremely literal translation of the poem, retaining the echoes of oral songs (see below, pp. 38–45), and made little or no attempt to recreate or replace the formal or prosodic features of the original. According to Joseph Greenberg, the existence of a prosodic system in a society depends on the possibility of making 'a numerical statement regarding the number of occurrences of the relevant characteristic in the line' ('A Survey of African Prosodic Systems', p. 927) in the verse sung or spoken in that society. The absence of such a system does not exclude the possibility that there are elements of play on speech sounds in the verse, it only means that such elements are not systematically used. Reduplication and alliteration are both common in Acoli oral literature and in *Wer pa Lawino*. There is reduplication in the word '*labutubutu*' in the refrain line '*Onang nang nango labutubutu*' from the women's song '*Abedo mera ata*' (below, p. 28), and in this line from the children's song '*Awii tolla*' (I make my own string): '*Tol ma kiwiyo ma kititino*', 'The strings I make are only small ones' (*Horn of My Love*, p. 36). It is very often used in *Wer pa Lawino*, both for emphasis and apparently to maintain a fairly consistent line length. In the following lines a number of examples are concentrated together:

Kono kiteitei peke lageng' geng'
Laboo cogo kor ma regerege
Kono bong' lutoro gutiya i ter munweng'
Ki bataniya i pyer ma negenege
Kono gomci peke la-um akic
Lageng' wang' cong' ma yegeyege
Kono peko dit, kono can i wic! (pp. 21–2)

[If there were no dresses to protect people, to wrap up bony breasts, if they didn't put sacks on their shrunk bottoms and blankets on weak waists, if there were no *busuti* to cover the waist, to cover up very crumbling knees, maybe things would be hard, maybe misery would reign.]

There is reduplication at the end of four of those seven lines, and although such a concentration of examples is unusual, the use of reduplication is common. There are two or three examples on most pages of the poem.

Alliteration is used in these lines from the children's song '*Awii tolla*':

Ogwal goyo bul,
An agoyo bul ni kiling,
Kiling, kiling, ki loko ca,

Ogwal beats the drum,
I also beat the drum, it goes 'kiling',
'Kiling, kiling' on the other side of the stream.
(*Horn of My Love*, p. 36)

These lines use the repetition of the soft-palatal plosive 'g' or 'k' to create a pleasure in sound which is an important feature of the song. This next song also gains considerable effect from alliteration:

Lut kot go cwara,
Go cwara,
Wekka meya;
Ee, wekka meya
Twolli tong cwara,
Tong cwara,
Wekka meya;
Ee, wekka meya:

Lightning, strike my husband,
Strike my husband,
Leave my lover;
Ee, leave my lover.
Snake, bite my husband,
Bite my husband,
Leave my lover,
Ee, leave my lover.
(*Horn of My Love*, p. 57)

The staccato effect of the short words is reinforced by the plosive 'k', 't' and 'g' in underlining the violence of the singer's mood. Her mood abruptly changes:

Nen ka woto,
Nenno mitta;
Neno ka myelo,
Nenno mitta;

See him walking,
How beautifully he walks;
See him dancing,
How beautifully he dances;
(loc. cit.)

The nasals 'n' and 'm' replace plosives as the dominant consonants and make the lines sound less harsh. The lines from *Wer pa Lawino* quoted (p. 25) show Okot's extensive use of alliteration in the Acoli version but he made no attempt to reproduce these elements in his translation of the poem. The constraints of translation seem to have adversely affected his ear for the sounds of English, since there is no alliteration in *Song of Lawino*, but it does occur in the later poems as this extract from 'Song of Malaya' illustrates:

Your eyes are black
With jealousy,
The veins of your neck
Are bursting with boiling blood.
Biting her lips,
Who is that brute . . . (p. 148)

One common element of verbal organization in oral songs which probably reflects the musical organization is the repetition of refrain lines at the end of a number of groups of lines, effectively dividing the songs into stanzas. The woman's satirical song '*Wan mon walony ku*' begins and ends with the three lines:

Wan mon walony ku,
Walony ku ki lok pa co;
Rac araca ki wor;

We women will never have peace,
We will never prosper, the troubles from men are ceaseless,
At night they are worse.
(*Horn of My Love*, p. 60)[9]

The line '*Rac araca ki wor*' is repeated five times more during the song. The song '*Abedo mera ataa*' expresses a similar emotion and uses the refrain line '*Onangnang nango labutubutu*' in a similar way:

Abedo mera ataa
Ka gwoko gang,
Atwom oneka ye,
Onangnang nango labutubutu;
Malaya otima nye,
Atworo toka ataa
Ka lilo ot,
Onangnang otima ba,
Onangnang nango labutubutu.

Here I am
Looking after my home,
The burden is killing me, oh;
And the suckers are sucking, lying on their beds.
The prostitutes treat me badly;
Here I am,
Making my house spotlessly clean,
The suckers treat me badly,
They are sucking, lying on their beds.
(*Horn of My Love*, p. 60)

In the next fifteen lines the refrain line occurs in a slightly modified form in every fifth line. The beginning of the line is altered, but the sounds '*nang*' and '*labutubutu*' are included each time. The song ends with a repetition of the refrain in its original form. Okot's use of the proverb '*Te Okono obur bong' luputu*' (The pumpkin in the old homestead must not be uprooted) which was also used in the 1956 version of the poem (see below, pp. 33–6), is a development of the use of refrain lines in oral songs. Apart from Section 14, where the proverb is the subject of the section and its implications are discussed (see below, pp. 38–40), it is used six times in the published version of *Wer pa Lawino* (pp. 12, 25, 42, 50, 60 and 146), providing a regular refrain except in Sections 7 to 12. In *Song of Lawino*, Section 14 has been left out and the proverb appears only four times (pp. 15, 30, 63 and 216).

In addition to refrain lines, some oral songs contain repetition of the same phrase in a number of lines in succession, as in these lines from a funeral song:

Anga ma neno kono pa meya?
Anga ma winyo bila pa meya?
Anga ma ngeyo wer pa meya?
Anga ma winyo bul pa meya?

But who can spot the headdress of my love?
Who can hear the sound of the horn of my love?
Who knows the song of my love?
Do you hear the drumming of my love?
(*Horn of My Love*, p. 122)

Okot sometimes uses a similar pattern in *Wer pa Lawino*, as in this description of the antics of Ocol and his friends at the ballroom dance:

Timme ducu lutimme Munu-Munu,
Ping'o lewic pe mako Munu,
Lukwako dako atyer, calo Munu
Luting'o pong' kor, calo Munu,
Wumato taa cigara calo Munu,
Wa mon, wa co calo Munu; (p. 31)

[It happens in everything that they behave in the white people's way for white people don't feel shame. They embrace each other's wives, like white people, they hold their chests close like white people. You smoke cigarettes, like white people, both men and women, like white people.]

The repetition of '*calo Munu*' continues for a further four lines. In the English version of the poem the repetition is considerably reduced. The line 'As white people do' occurs only three times, though most of the indictment of white people's ways of dancing and kissing is translated.

If we accept Okot's suggestion, that music should be considered the feature that distinguishes verse from prose in Acoli oral literature (see above, p. 6), then he is, in *Wer pa Lawino*, a pioneer of Acoli unsung verse. The lines he uses are considerably longer and much more consistent in length than are the lines in oral songs. They vary between about eight and thirteen syllables in different parts of the poem and are most commonly about nine or ten syllables. The major organizing principle he has chosen is that of rhyme, which is a feature alien to Acoli unsung verse. The poem is written in an irregular *ab ab* rhyming pattern, as in this example:

Cwara ka oera ng'allo Acol,
Timme iwacci min gweno
Ma car, ma myero luum i kigol.
Delle ma wang'e obok-aboka
Ma wang'e calo wang' guu'
Timme calo lawaro mupok-apoka
Ma ger ataa calo ng'uu: (p. 13)

> [When my husband starts mocking black people, he acts like a mother hen that is careless, that should be covered by a basket. His eyes go red with anger. His eyes are like the eyes of a beast. He acts like a mad hyena, he is needlessly fierce, like a beast of prey.]

This disciplined verse form, with its new controlling features of line length and rhyme supplemented by the embellishments of alliteration and reduplication borrowed from oral literature, is in marked contrast to the irregular free verse of the English poem. There is no rhyme and no consistent stress pattern in the verse in *Song of Lawino*. The line division often leads to a strong emphasis on the last syllable of the line or the penultimate syllable:

A loaf in a half-gourd
Returns its heat
And does not become wet
In the bottom;
And the earthen dish
Keeps the gravy hot
And the meat steaming (pp. 76–7)

The basic line in Okot's later poems is of four to six syllables and very short lines are the commonest variations. These shorter lines produce a faster-moving verse than *Song of Lawino* and the very short lines break the verse up and change its pace, producing a rhythm that is jerky and bouncing:

You sister
From Pokot
Who grew in the open air,
You are fresh . . .
Ah!
Come
Walk with me
In the City gardens,
(*Song of Ocol*, p. 53)

Okot avoids the cluttering of the beginnings of his lines by cutting out the repetition of structural words which is common in *Song of Lawino*, as these two descriptions of the symptoms of a sick child show. First, from *Song of Lawino*:

And all the youthful diseases
Run after him
As if he was a beautiful girl,

So that he has coughs and dysentery
And throat trouble and eye sickness,
And his ears have pus
And his legs have ulcers
And he is bony, skinny,
And his loin-string is loose, (pp. 161–2)

This contrasts with this one from *Song of Ocol*:

That child lying
On the earth
Numb
Bombs exploding in his head,
Blood boiling
Heavy with malarial parasites
Raging through his veins, (pp. 25–8)

The more concise description in *Song of Ocol* is more effective.

Okot confessed to the inadequacy of his translation in relation to prosody on the back of the title page of *Song of Lawino*:

> Translated from the Acoli by the author who has thus clipped a bit of the eagle's wings and rendered the sharp edges of the warrior's sword rusty and blunt and has also murdered rhythm and rhyme.

Gerald Moore also noticed the importance of the effects that have been lost:

> Translation has presented the poet with painful problems. Rhyme, assonance and tonal variation, the chief ornaments of the original text, are lost. (Gerald Moore, 'Grasslands Poetry', a review of *Song of Lawino*, in *Transition*, p. 53)

Okot's evident skill in creating a vigorous workable form for Acoli written verse is in no way reflected in *Song of Lawino* and this is a considerable loss to non-Acoli readers. The overall formal organization of the poem, however, displays a similar skill in adapting traditional techniques to new situations. Timothy Wangusa noted that 'the formal organization of the poem is in a class of its own' and that its 'internal structure is that of a dialogue or a debate (Timothy Wangusa, 'East African Poetry', in Eldred Jones (ed.), *African Literature Today, No. 6, Poetry in Africa*, p. 46). He did not point out how the use of apostrophe by Okot establishes the roles of the participants, sets up the atmosphere of debate, and contributes to the tone of voice used by the singers.

Critics have pointed out the role of traditional imagery in Okot's poems,[10] and this is important, but it does not explain the difference in style between Okot and poets like Okigbo or Soyinka who also borrow images from their own oral tradition. The particular way in which Okot uses apostrophe contributes a great deal to the unique manner of his poetry.

Notes to Chapter 2

1. Okot p'Bitek. *Two Songs* (Nairobi: East African Publishing House, 1971), p. 12. All further page references to *Two Songs* are to the same edition. (See bibliography.)
2. Okot p'Bitek, *Wer pa Lawino* (Nairobi: East African Publishing House, 1969), p. 38. The Acoli is literally: 'Ocol, friend, you speak nonsense, in the past you saw me as I am still.' All further page references to *Wer pa Lawino* are to the same edition. (See bibliography.) Throughout the book all my own translations from Acoli that are used in the text are in square brackets, while Okot's verse translations are presented as quotations with a page reference or a note indicating their source.
3. Section 6 of *Wer pa Lawino* has a markedly different ending; see below p. 37.
4. Literally: 'how many *bwola* songs can you play?' (on the drum).
5. No equivalent in *Song of Lawino*.
6. '*La-coo*' is not translated, '*Wod-wegi*' is literally 'Son of your father'.
7. '*Rwot*' is literally 'Chief'.
8. For a comparison with the end of the Acoli version see below pp. 38–41.
9. Part of this song is quoted and discussed below, p. 98.
10. For example: 'Unfettered, Unfree', a review of *Song of Lawino*, in *The Times Literary Supplement*, 16 February 1967, p. 125: 'Much of the imagery is rooted in their traditional songs of love, war, victory and death.' Timothy Wangusa, op. cit., p. 47: '. . . the images are prescribed by the village'. The use of imagery borrowed from traditional literature is discussed below, pp. 46–55.

3 Three Versions of Lawino's 'Song'

THE English version of *Song of Lawino* is a translation of a poem that had been expanded from the thirty pages of typescript of the 1956 version into a poem of 140 printed pages, completed some ten years later.[1] The later Acoli version of the poem is a more complex and better thought-out poem but it is also farther removed from Acoli oral tradition in method and in content as well as in length. While in most respects *Song of Lawino* is a translation of *Wer pa Lawino*, in one or two ways reorganization in the translation appears to be a continuation of the principles that were used in the rewriting of the Acoli poem. This chapter compares the three versions of the poem, showing the radical changes made in the expansion of the Acoli original and the relatively minor structural changes that went with translation, and illustrates the literal method of translation used for most of the poem.

The 1956 *Wer pa Lawino* is divided into twenty-one sections, each with a short title, for example:

> *Lawino ngeyo kit yen ma pol* (Section 5)
>
> [Lawino knows many kinds of firewood]

or:

> *Lawino maro atabo lobo ki awal* (Section 6)
>
> [Lawino likes the clay pot and the calabash][2]

The length of the sections varies from thirteen or fourteen lines to nearly five pages, the sections tending to grow longer towards the end of the poem, whereas in the published poem there are fourteen sections and the shortest is nearly as long as the longest in the 1956 poem. There is no correspondence in the sequence of ideas in the two poems, although there are a few identical lines at the beginning of the poems, and the final section of the 1956 poem, called '*Lawino koko Ocol*' (Lawino cries for Ocol), corresponds in some ways to Section 12 of the published poem. Some of its lines have been retained, for example:

I kare ca Ocol pud dano . . .
Onongo cwara Ocol pud Acol
Wod pa twon onongo pud Acoli
Wod pa Agik, nya jo Okol
Onongo pud Acol pud Acoli . . . (pp. 135–6)

[In those days when Ocol was still a person . . . when Ocol my husband was still a black man, the son of a Bull was still Acoli, the son of Agik, the daughter of the people of Okol, was still a black man, still Acoli . . .]

Lawino's tears for Ocol also anticipate her request to the clansmen to mourn over the 'death' of her husband.

Despite the reorganization, most of the main ideas and a fair number of the words of the original are used in the published poem. Some of the material on Western and Acoli dances which occurs in Section 3 of the published version (*Wer pa Lawino*, pp. 27–35; cf. *Song of Lawino*, pp. 31–41) comes from the contrast in Section 16 and 17 of the 1956 poem. Lawino confesses ignorance of Western dances in a section headed '*Lawino pe ngeyo dok pe mito myel Munu*' (Lawino doesn't know and doesn't like white men's dances), and remembers her skill in Acoli dances in the next one: '*Lawino yang' onongo Rwot Bulu*' (Lawino used to be Drum Chief). Lawino's nostalgia for the time when Ocol was wooing her (*Wer pa Lawino*, pp. 37–8; cf. *Song of Lawino*, pp. 44–5) was present in Section 15 of the original, which was headed '*Lawino pwoyo wi cwara pi kare ma con, kare ma onongo Lawino pudi*' (Lawino reminds her husband of the time before, when she was still Lawino). Her attack on Ocol's ignorance of Acoli games and dances (*Wer pa Lawino*, pp. 41–2; cf. *Song of Lawino*, pp. 48–9) was prefigured in Section 18 of the 1956 version. The 1956 version had a section on hair styles, Section 20, which included the lines:

Yubbu wiya Munu-munu ngaya,
Pingo Maa Acoli pe nya Munu
Opwonya deyo Acoli pe pa Munu.
(cf. *Wer pa Lawino*, pp. 43–4; *Song of Lawino*, p. 52)

[To do my hair in a white woman's way is not easy because my mother is Acoli and not the daughter of a white man. She taught me Acoli adornments, not those of white people.]

By far the most thoroughly covered subject in the 1956 version is the contrast between European and Acoli habits of cooking and eating which occupies Sections 2 to 8. Comparatively little of the material in the later sections of the published version appears in the 1956 poem.[3]

The first section of the 1956 poem shows how thoroughly even those parts of the poem which have been used in the published version have been reorganized and expanded as they were transferred from one version to the other. The first five lines of both versions are almost identical, the only change in the published poem being the substitution of '*Wod-wegi*' (Son of your father) for '*Omera*' (Brother) in the fourth line:

Cwara kadi pud icaya,
La-coo, kadi pud inywara
Ya an akwanyo caro pa waya;
Omera, kadi pud ipora
Ki yugi ma tye i wi odur . . .
(*Wer pa Lawino*, p. 11; cf. *Song of Lawino*, p. 13)

[My husband, though you still despise me, man, though you still scorn me that I have picked up the stupidity of my aunt; my brother, though you still compare me with the rubbish that is in the rubbish pit . . .]

Thereafter the published version begins to elaborate ideas a little more. Here is the remainder of the first section of the 1956 poem '*Lawino lego cware Ocol owek yet*' (Lawino begs her husband Ocol to stop the insults) opposite the next nine lines of the published poem:

(1956)

Wat-wa kadi pud iyeta
Ki dum Munu, kun inyatte
Iwacci in pe imita,
Kun iloko ma ingatte:
   Ya pe ang'eyo wa ki 'a'
   Pien pe akwano i cukuru
Gwokke; naka akwiya 'b'
Lokki mita kato um ukuru
Gwokke naka akwiya 'u'
ENTO TE OKONO PE LUPUTU

[Our relative, although
you still insult me with
the language of the white
man, while you brag and
say that you don't want me.
You speak to show off:
   That I don't even know

(1969)

Ilanya, ipako ya bong'imita
Ya arom ki gigu ma wi obur
Iyeta, ibuku dogi ki buru
Ya bong' angeyo wa ki 'a'
Ya bong' akwano i cukuru
Ni an pe amako nying'a
Ipora ki la-gwok kurukuru;
Gwokke larema, la-lwak omera,
Gwok lebi jal, gwok dogi;
(*Wer pa Lawino*, pp. 11–12; cf.
Song of Lawino, pp. 13–14)

[You reject me, you say that
you do not want me, that I am
equal to the things left in
the deserted site of a village,
you abuse me, you insult me
very badly that I do not know

'a' because I didn't
read in school
Take care, I shall always
be ignorant of 'b'. Your
words want to outdo the
noise of a puppy.
Take care, I shall always
be ignorant of 'u',
BUT DON'T UPROOT THE
PUMPKIN]

as far as 'a' that I didn't read
in school, that I haven't been
baptized. You compare me with
a little dog, a puppy. Be
careful my friend, age-mate
of my brother, Guard your
tongue fellow, guard your mouth.]

Both versions contain the same reported insult relating to Lawino's lack of schooling and both contain the same tone of warning in preparation for a counterattack from Lawino. The 1956 version also contains some ideas which appear later in the section in the published poem, the proverb '*ento te okono pe luputu*' (but don't uproot the pumpkin) occurs in the published version thirteen lines later and the words '*Yeta ki dum Munu*' (He insults me with the language of the white man) comes a few lines below that (p. 12).

In addition to this reorganization and rewriting, a number of new elements have been introduced most of which increase the satiric impact of the poem through an extension of the fictional elements in it.[4] The 1956 poem is considerably more defensive in its cultural contrasts, recounting *kit Acoli* (Acoli customs) with only minimal contrasts with *kit Munu* (white man's customs) in most cases. The most important new element in the early sections of the published poem is the character of Kelementina, the major focus for satirical descriptions of *kit Munu* in a number of passages relating to women's fashions. Most of the material in Sections 7 and 10 and the whole of Sections 8, 9 and 11 are new. These new parts include the description of Ocol's behaviour in the home in Section 7, the whole of Lawino's description of the missionaries and their education, the speculation about the creation myth, Lawino's relation of the religious practices of the Acoli, and the whole of the description of post-Independence politics. It is in these sections that most of the anecdotes that give us a fuller picture of Ocol and Lawino occur, and these are the sections in which the rhetoric of Acoli songs has least influenced Okot, as they are in the third person throughout and contain only one example of apostrophe (*Wer pa Lawino*, p. 72; *Song of Lawino*, p. 97). These new parts make the published poem effectively a new poem rather than an expanded version of the older one.

In one or two ways, minor changes introduced into *Wer pa Lawino* during its translation into English can be regarded as further movements in the same direction as changes made to the 1956 version of the poem. The most drastic reorganization concerns Section 6 of the 1969 *Wer pa Lawino* which collects together the material on cooking and eating habits from seven short sections in the 1956 poem. There is a tendency for those parts of the section dealing with *kit Acoli* to become a dull catalogue of eating and cooking habits. In the English version of the poem Okot has corrected this. He has gathered together at the beginning of the section all the elements concerned with *kit Munu* and he has held together the descriptions of *kit Acoli* by his description of Lawino's mother's house. This description, from: 'Come, brother, / Come into my mother's house' to the mention of Lawino singing with her sister (pp. 71–4) has no equivalent in *Wer pa Lawino*. Okot uses the remainder of the description of the house to link together various ideas Lawino has about cooking and eating in a coherent way. The end of the section from 'Ocol says / Black people's foods are primitive', including the extract from the song (pp. 79–80), is also new in the English translation of the poem. The translation misses out many details about cooking and eating habits which Okot retained from the 1956 version of *Wer pa Lawino*. Particularly where he is describing *kit Acoli*, there is more loss of detail in the translation than is usual in other parts of the poem. The overall effect of these changes is to make the English version of this section a more coherent and less repetitive section than that in *Wer pa Lawino*.

Section 10 of *Song of Lawino* contains some new elements which sharpen and clarify Lawino's reflection of the character of Acoli religion that Okot describes in *Religion of the Central Luo*.[5] In both versions, the 1969 *Wer pa Lawino* and the English poem, Lawino complains that Ocol attacks her belief in the kite with the flame in its anus, but only in the English version does she go on to compare this belief to Ocol's belief in angels: 'The beautiful men / With the wings of vultures' (p. 153; cf. *Wer pa Lawino*, p. 109). Similarly, in both versions Lawino complains that though Ocol wears a crucifix and his daughters wear rosaries, he doesn't accept the use of Acoli charms, but only in the English poem does she reinforce this comparison with the short anecdote of the superstitious behaviour of the nun who was afraid of 'A large snake' (p. 156; cf. *Wer pa Lawino*, pp. 109–10). The most important addition to the section comes at the end. The last three pages of the English version from 'It is true / White man's medicines are strong,' are new material and these include the reference to 'the journey to Pagak' and to 'Mother Death' (pp. 172–4), the ideas which illustrate the fatalistic agnosticism of the Central Luo in the face of the biggest tragedies of life which Okot very strongly asserts to be an important feature of their religious life in his study (Religion of the Central Luo, pp. 154–60; also see below, pp. 137–8).

The elements of dialogue, supported by the rhetoric of apostrophe (see above, pp. 19–21), are the main structural links between *Song of Lawino* and oral tradition and these aspects of the poem are substantially modified by passages of descriptive poetry and anecdotes, some of which were introduced and all expanded in later versions of the poem. Apart from the description in Section 6, whose function has just been discussed above (p. 37), the beginning of Section 2, which describes Clementine's use of cosmetics (pp. 22–4) and the bulk of Sections 3 and 5, contrasting *kit Acoli* and *kit Munu* in relation to dancing and to hair styles (*Song of Lawino*, pp. 31–41 and 51–63), are descriptive poetry. On many other occasions, Lawino illustrates her debating points with anecdotes of her past, some of which are generalized accounts of what happened on a particular set of occasions, like the description of the times Ocol came to woo Lawino near the beginning of Section 4 (pp. 44–5), or her account of his behaviour when he 'Is reading a new book' (pp. 92–3). In Sections 9 and 11 such anecdotes provide the framework of the section. Lawino's unresolved speculations on the problem of the creation arise out of her account of how the priests never wait 'To answer even one question' (p. 134), and her more vivid description of Ocol's behaviour when she questions him (pp. 140–2). Her attack on the conduct of politics is constructed around three generalized pictures of the way Ocol behaves as a politician in particular situations, first the busy pre-election period when he '. . . roams the countryside / Like a wild goat' (p. 179), then his behaviour when the party leaders come, and finally a typical scene at one of his political speeches in his constituency (pp. 191–4). Section 8 of the poem devotes more than half of its space to two anecdotes of particular occasions from Lawino's past. First, she describes the Sunday she visited the Protestant Church and ran away when the people were called forward to 'eat people' (pp. 114–15), and she follows that with the much longer description of the evening when she ran away from the Catholic Evening Speakers' Class to join the dancers in the 'get-stuck' dance (pp. 115–23), which is extended by the account of the teacher joining in with them and trying to whisper to Lawino (pp. 124–5). These anecdotes extend the range of subject matter of the poem and vary its tone a good deal but they also remove it a little from the elements of oral tradition which give the poem its overall shape.

Song of Lawino is very much closer to the 1969 version of *Wer pa Lawino* than is the 1956 poem and must be regarded as a translation rather than a new poem. Apart from the reorganization and the new additions to Sections 6 and 10, the only other major change between the two poems concerns the omission of Section 14 and some minor changes in Section 13 of the English poem. Section 14 of *Wer pa Lawino* is an elaboration and an explanation of the proverb '*Te Okono pe Luputu*'. The significance of this proverb arises from the semi-nomadic period of Acoli history when there were frequent migrations of individual clans within the area of Acoliland in search of more fertile land or because of wars or disputes within a chiefdom (see below, p. 103). In these circumstances pumpkins often grew wild on the sites of settlements that had been deserted and these pumpkins would be left to grow by anyone who passed through the area because to destroy them '. . . would be merely purposeless destruction of food stuff' ('Oral Literature Among the Acoli and Lang'o', p. 373). Okot explains the social meaning of the proverb in this way:

> Old customs which are harmless and may even be useful, should not be uprooted. It is used a great deal by old men who feel that the young educated men may throw the entire Acoli culture overboard.
> (loc. cit.)

Lawino begins Section 14 by reminding Ocol of this:

Te Okono obur bong' luputu
Ka itwon doo tere adoya
Ony cet dyel ki cet tutu
Bong' iwek kweri okati, koo-akoya;
Ka iwod woru atika-tika
Put lum, Okono ng'oo-ang'oya;
Puttu Okono tal, lik-alika . . .
Te Okono obur bong' luputu
Ping'o meno cam pe gi-tuku'
Kadi iyeng' ma teri oduttu.
Labal cam pwoyo luyok kore ki luduku! (pp. 147–8)

> [The pumpkin in the old homestead may not be uprooted. If you are really a bull, weed it, manure it, pour the dung of goats and the refuse of waste salt on it, don't let the hoe cut it. If you are truly the son of your father uproot the grass, leave the pumpkin alone; to cut it is wizardry . . . The pumpkin in the old homestead may not be uprooted because that is food; it is not to be played with: although you are satisfied with your bottom swelling, anyone who spoils food will be hit in the chest with the butt of a gun.]

She continues to elaborate on the same theme, that '*Okono cam pe gi-tuku*' (the pumpkin is a food not a plaything) and uses the same image to suggest to Ocol that his present prosperity may not last for ever, he may be one of those who never reaches the new homestead:

Kadi iyeng', kadi piny oyutu!
Too kec lit loyo too luduku!
Joo ma oo i gony nok;
Can ka bino pe kong' tito:
Turu dano calo ng'ok gwok
Bong' bino ikare ma imito. (p. 149)

[Even if you are satisfied, even if darkness falls, death from hunger is painful, it is worse than death by gunshot. Few people manage to reach their new homestead. When misery is coming it never tells people, it surprises or comes suddenly like the vomit of a dog, it doesn't come at the time when you want it.]

She elaborates on the dangerous folly in his destructive conduct in relation to necessary things in the homestead and then ends with the most general summary in the poem of her views as to the future of Acoliland:

Pi dong'o pa lobo an ayee,
Lobo tua opwoyo ocit anyim
Pii bong' mol dok odyee;
Dano bong' bedo calo gi-tim.
Ento yat madit pwoyo ocwal lyake i ng'om,
Ma tut, ka wek ocir lapiru.
Ma onyong'o anyong'a, ka ng'om yom
Ka yamo kot obino, bong' kuru.
TE OKONO OBUR BONG' LUPUTU.
OKONO WI OBUR BONG' LUPUTU
OKONO BONG' LUPUTU! (p. 151)

[As for the development of the land, I accept our land had better go before the rest. A river does not flow back to its source, people don't behave like wild animals. But a strong tree must have strong deep roots in the ground if it is to struggle and stand against a whirlwind. That which squats only on the surface, when the ground is soft and when the storm wind comes, it does not withstand it. THE PUMPKIN IN THE OLD HOMESTEAD MUST NOT BE UPROOTED, THE PUMPKIN IN THE OLD HOMESTEAD MUST NOT BE UPROOTED, DON'T UPROOT THE PUMPKIN.]

The omission of this section from the English version of the poem substantially changes the emphasis of that ending, especially in relation to the importance of Lawino's rivalry with Clementine (see below, pp. 67–70).

The end of Section 13 in both published poems revives the idea of Lawino's rivalry with Clementine, which has not been mentioned since Section 5, as Lawino refers to Clementine again, when she says '*Wil bong'o jara ki nyeka,*' 'Buy clothes for the woman / With whom I share you' and goes on to ask Ocol to '*miya kare*', 'give me one chance' to show him '*lonyo ma i odo*' (pp. 145–6), 'the wealth in your house' (pp. 215–16), presumably with the hope of at last winning back his affection. The reminder of this rivalry ties together the beginning of the poem and the later anecdotal sections where Clementine is not mentioned, but to make this the end of the whole poem gives the rivalry with Clementine much more emphasis than it has in the Acoli version. In *Song of Lawino* the image of the threatening whirlwind that ends *Wer pa Lawino* (see p. 40) occurs in Section 13 in a less specific form. Lawino says:

When you took the axe
And threatened to cut the *Okango*
That grows on the ancestral shrine
You were threatening
To cut yourself loose,
To be tossed by the winds
This way and that way. (p. 214)

This paragraph has no equivalent in the Acoli version; as a substitute for the reference to the whirlwind in the last paragraph of the Acoli version it is inadequate as it is less generalized in its implications, containing the same shift from the public concerns which end *Wer pa Lawino* to the related private concerns which is implicit in allowing the rivalry with Clementine to end the poem. The English version also lacks any general statement about '*dong'o pa lobo*' (the development of the land) like that quoted above (see p. 40) and the proverbial didactic tone of Section 14 in the Acoli has no equivalent in the English poem which therefore ends with Lawino in a much humbler and more pleading relationship with Ocol.

There are no other parts of the poem where the translation is significantly different from the original although there are minor changes in many parts of the poem, most often involving the omission of illustrative detail in the translation. In this passage from the end of Section 2, the Acoli version of the poem has been considerably reduced in the translation but its contribution to the meaning of the whole poem has hardly been altered. The equivalent passage from *Song of Lawino* is placed next to a literal translation for comparison:

Ento alego Ocol owek yet
Cwara owek alany ki caro,
Owek kano wiye te ywet,
Owek babbe, ki lok ni an la-caaro,
Ka yetto dano ribbo ki megi-gi,
Ka cayo kit pa Acol ni col,
Owek pang'ng'e ni-pang'-pang' i pa ji
Pien weko minne nen calo la-wol,
Miyo lunyodo-ne nen calo pagaji! (pp. 24–5)

[But I beg Ocol to stop the insults, my husband should stop foolishness and contempt, stop hiding his head in his armpit, stop deceiving himself, with this idea that I am primitive. When he insults people together with their mothers, when he despises the customs of black men that they are dirty, he should stop fooling himself by turning to the ways of other peoples because he makes his mother appear as a witch, he gives the impression that his parents are slaves.]

All I ask
Is that my husband should
stop the insults,
My husband should refrain
From heaping abuses on
my head.
He should stop being half-
crazy,
And saying terrible things
about my mother. (p. 29)

The details missed out include an untranslatable idiom: '*Owek kano wiye te ywet*' (stop hiding his head in his armpit) which emphasizes the idea of self-deception and some illustration of what Lawino means by the 'insults' of her and the 'abuses' of her mother, which in the original were directed by Ocol at his own parents. Nothing of substance is missed out and, as the details of his insults repeat those elsewhere in the poem, only the loss of the idiomatic expression and the loss of the play on sounds involve any diminution in the impact of the passage. Less frequently there is a slight expansion in the English version in the description of things Acoli which are unfamiliar to a wider audience, as in this description of the things Ocol admired in Lawino's mother's house when he was wooing her:

In yang' ineno wino bada
Ma lutuku ki diro me Acoli,
Ot-wa lutado ki lagada
Abaa ogero ki ryeko me Acoli;
Ceng'ineno tiko pyer lamera,
Maa orubu ki diro me Acoli,
Komi yang' myel pi kedo kora,
Kedo pyera ki wang' nak laka. (p. 38)

[In the past you saw the giraffe-hair bracelets of my arm that were made carefully with the skill of the Acoli, our house is woven with flat reed stalks,

You loved my giraffe-tail bangles
My father bought them for me
From the Hills in the East
The roof of my mother's house
Was beautifully laced
With elephant grass;

my father built it with the
genius of the Acoli; in
those days you saw the
waist beads of my sister,
that my mother threaded
with the skill of the Acoli.
Your body used to tremble
for the tattoos on my breasts,
the tattoos on my loins
and the gap in my teeth.]

My father built it
With the skill of the Acoli
You admired my sister's
Colourful ten-stringed loin
beads;
My mother threaded them
And arranged them with care.
You trembled
When you saw the tattoos
On my breasts
And the tattoos below my
belly button;
And you were very fond
Of the gap in my teeth! (p. 45)

Okot has changed the detail about the giraffe-tail bracelet by mentioning the mountain in the East, he has missed out the repeated line '*ki diro me Acoli*' or '*ki ryeko me Acoli*' (with the skill or wisdom of the Acoli), using it only once, and added a little explanation to the mention of the building of the house and the making of the loin beads, things which are a little unfamiliar to non-Acoli readers.

Despite these modifications, *Song of Lawino* is essentially a very literal translation of *Wer pa Lawino*; in many parts of the poem it is difficult to produce a more literal translation. This passage from Section 3, for example follows the original extremely closely:

Myel pa lu-rok adaa akwiya,
Ruk pa lu-rok pe ang'eyo,
Wa tuku tugi ducu pud ng'aya;
An ang'eyo myel tua me deyo.
I myel rumma adaa an adanya,
Ma yang' onyutta myel Acoli
Akwiya myel Munu, myel banya;
Myel camba akwiya, pe abwoli. (p. 27)

[It is true that I do not know
the dances of foreigners, I do
not know the dress of foreigners,
even their games defeat me. I
know our dances with pride. It
is true, in the rumba dance I
am clumsy. In the past my mother

It is true
I am ignorant of the dances of
foreigners
And how they dress
I do not know.
Their games
I cannot play,

showed me Acoli dances, I am ignorant of white people's dances, the barn dance, the samba dance, I am ignorant of them, I don't deceive you.]

I only know the dances of our
people.
I cannot dance the rumba,
My mother taught me
The beautiful dances of
Acoli.
I do not know the dances of
White People.
I will not deceive you,
I cannot dance the samba! (pp. 31–2)

All the quotations which compare English and Acoli versions illustrate the relative economy of the Acoli language as compared to English. This springs partly from its use of subject prefixes (for example '*i*-neno'—*you* saw) and object suffixes ('Ocol deg-*a*'—Ocol hates *me*) with the verb, and possessive suffixes with nouns ('cwara'—*my* husband), and the lack of auxiliary verbs in Acoli. These and other features of the language make it inevitably more economical than English but Okot has made this difference appear greater by the comparative shortness of the lines in *Song of Lawino*; thus the two lines 'When you saw the tattoos / On my breasts' translate the three words '*pi kedo kora*' (for tattoos of my breasts). *Song of Lawino* therefore appears to be a considerably longer poem than *Wer pa Lawino* when in fact more has been dropped from the Acoli poem than added to it.

Notes to Chapter 3

1. Okot has said in conversation that the published version of *Wer pa Lawino* was ready for publication in 1966 when the English version was published, the delay in publication (until 1969) being the responsibility of the publisher.
2. A copy of the 1956 version of *Wer pa Lawino* is available for restricted use in the library of the University of Nairobi. All quotations from that poem in this chapter are taken from that copy.
3. But Lawino does question Ocol's obsessive concern with doing things by the clock in Section 13 of the 1956 poem, which is called '*Pi gwokko Cawa*' (For being careful about time) and includes the lines '*Ka latin kok, mii odoti*' (When a child cries, it is given the breast to suck), the title of Section 7 in the

published poem. Section 14 of the 1956 poem deals with '*Aijini*' (hygiene), a topic raised near the beginning of Section 10 of the later version.

4. For a discussion of these fictional elements, see below, pp. 62–72.
5. For a discussion of how Lawino's ideas reflect Okot's in that book, see below, pp. 136–8.

4 Verbal Echoes

IN addition to its use of some rhetorical and prosodic devices from oral songs, *Wer pa Lawino* borrowed from oral literature in its use of proverbs and idioms and in verbal echoes of the songs. The use Okot made of artefacts like the spear and horn in his poems reflects their social importance in Acoli life and also their symbolic value in oral literature. These aspects of his poem presented major problems to him as a translator. He has dealt with some of these difficulties simply by leaving out problematic idioms and in other places his method of translation has caused obscurity, but on the whole his extremely literal translations retain the proverbial and symbolic content of the original. In some instances he has deliberately chosen an over-literal or archaic translation to illustrate a particular idea about social change. In these respects his method of translation is the best he could have chosen to enable the English poem to carry the ideas about society he wishes to put across.

There are a number of proverbs in Section 11 of the poem. Four are used in connection with the relationships between Ocol, his brother, and Lawino, two of them refer to the former closeness of the two brothers:

> *Onong'o gin um ki wang', gicalo rudi!*
> *Onong'o gipoko pyer ng'wen!* (p. 126)

> They were as close to each other
> As the eye and the nose,
> They were like twins,
> And they shared everything
> Even a single white ant. (p. 184)

The reference to '*um ki wang*' (nose and eyes) is proverbial and needs the extra line of explanation that Okot gives ('they were as close to each other'); a literal translation would be simply 'they were nose and eyes'. The other '*gipoko pyer ng'wen*' (they wivide an ant between them) is a little more self-explanatory, though again Okot adds a non-figurative explanation ('they shared everything') to make sure the proverb is understood. Another proverb is used to express their present hostility in the strongest possible terms when Lawino says:

Ocol bong' giribo kwon gikwed ominne!
Wa pii giribo ma i kulu! (p. 125)

Ocol does not share
Millet bread with his brother,
Water from the public well
Is the only thing they share! (p. 182)

In this case the translation is literal, the proverb '*pii giribo ma i kulu*' (they share only water from the well) is self-explanatory. Lawino is referring to a proverb which is used to emphasize the dangers in relationship of a man's brother to his wife when she says '*pe ya ni oree biketto latin*' (p. 129), 'Not that joking may cause pregnancy' (p. 182). In this case there is no addition to the translation to make the proverbial meaning clear and the point of the phrase in the English poem remains obscure, though its superficial meaning is clear. Okot also uses a proverb to describe Ocol's fawning behaviour in front of the party leaders; Lawino says:

'*Rwot ineka*' *calo pe* '*Rwot ineka*' (p. 129)

He says to the bosses
'O Chief you kill me with laughter!' (p. 191)

The English is again expanded a little to clarify the proverb which is used in its short form '*Rwot ineka*' (Chief you kill me) the laughter being understood.[1]

The most obvious influence of the verbal content of oral songs on both published versions of *Song of Lawino* is the presence of acknowledged borrowings, the indented quotations that Lawino uses to illustrate *kit Acoli* in many respects. Though there are slight changes in the songs used (cf. *Wer pa Lawino*, pp. 94 and 138; *Song of Lawino*, pp. 130 and 203), there is no marked difference in the way in which the indented quotations are used between the two published versions. In addition to these indented quotations, Lawino's words frequently echo the words of songs. When she says that '*Lok wai lit loyo odoo!*' (p. 13), 'Words cut more painfully than sticks!' (p. 16), she is echoing the words of an *orak* song of the 1940s: '*Kop loyo ado*', (Words pain more than a stick; 'Oral Literature Among the Acoli and Lang'o', p. 287). Similarly, in the nostalgia for the time when Ocol was wooing her, she says:

Ce ceng' pud wabedo atena, (p. 19)

. . . only recently
We would sit close together, touching each other! (p. 21)

There is a funeral song which begins '*Ceng pud bedo / Gikwed cware atena*' (She used to sit close to her husband, touching each other; *Horn of My Love*, p. 136). Lawino's references to burst eyeballs are an elaboration of the image in this *orak* song against a teacher:

Wange otoo wa con,
Polo nen ki iye;
Too wang lapwony,
Polo nen do;
Wange otoo con;
Lapwony weko maraya ku;
Wange otoo con,
Polo nen ki iye.

His eyes died long ago,
You can see clouds in them;
The death of the eyes of the teacher,
Clouds are visible in them, oh;
His eyes died long ago;
The teacher does not leave his glasses behind;
His eyes died long ago,
You can see clouds in them.
(*Horn of My Love*, p. 76)

The teacher's spectacles enable him to read the white man's books but they never leave his face so that his eyes are dead to all else around him and the vague clouds of his learning are reflected in them. In *Song of Lawino*, Lawino rounds off her condemnation of Ocol for his incompetence in Acoli games, songs, and dances by saying that 'the dark glasses . . . cover up / The husks of exploded eye balls' (p. 49; cf. *Wer pa Lawino*, pp. 41–2). This idea occurs for the first time in *Wer pa Lawino* and is repeated in Section 12 of *Song of Lawino* when Lawino says that, in Ocol's house,

Col piny mwoco tong' wang' (p. 138)

. . . the boiling darkness
Bursts your eye balls. (p. 202)

Both versions of the poem take up the idea again in Section 13 when Lawino talks of removing the blood clotted on his eyes and getting rid of his blindness (*Wer pa Lawino*, p. 144; *Song of Lawino*, p. 211). In these examples Okot's imagination has been influenced by oral tradition whether or not he was aware of that influence.

Okot's use of the words '*bila*' (horn), '*twon*' (bull) and '*tong*' (spear) reflect their social importance and their use in oral literature. Every Acoli young man in the countryside has a horn on which he can produce his own personal note or group of notes so that he can be identified from a long way off by those who know him. He will blow the horn to signal his position to others during a hunt or in battle and after the battle the notes of the horn tell the women of victory before they see their men. His horn thus represents a young man's individuality and his reputation. In a number of funeral songs, the memory of the notes of a young man's horn is a main element in the nostalgia of the mourners, as in this sister's lament:

En acel loo woko do;
Omera kutu kiliko ye;
Twon co wa dong peke.
Nyodo Alal okutu bila,
Ineno nyoda pa Alal
Yam okutu bila wi jobi;
Omera kutu wi laro ye;
Ee, en acel loo woko do!

The only son of my mother has melted away, oh;
My brother used to blow his flute;
Our bull of men is no more.
Son of Alal blew his horn,
Son of Alal used to blow his horn,
Ee, he blew his horn standing atop the buffalo that he had killed;
My brother used to blow his horn from the hill top, oh.
The only son of my mother has melted away, oh!
(*Horn of My Love*, p. 131)[2]

When discussing the arbitrary way in which death strikes, Lawino uses the horn to contrast the celebration of the majority of the clan after a victorious battle with the mourning of those who have lost a son. The others come home 'Blowing their horns, loud and clear!' whilst you sing songs of mourning for the dead (p. 164). Similarly, in the contrast she draws between winners and losers in political competition, Lawino talks of '*bila ki tum bedo li-wiir*' (p. 128),[3] the 'horns loud and proud!' (p. 189) of the victors contrasted with the silence of the defeated. The name of a person may spread beyond those places where he is physically present, just as the horn announces a young man to those who cannot see him. Thus Lawino tells us:

Nying'a onong'o kutu i Payira, (p. 38)

. . . my name blew
Like a horn
Among the Payira. (p. 44)

In contrast to Lawino, who earned her reputation, Ocol has lost fame that was handed down to him:

Ce yang' nying' Gang tua kutu! (p. 141)[4]

Your grandfather was a Bull among men
And although he died long ago
His name still blows like a horn, (p. 206)

The title '*twon*' (bull) is a compliment to courage and a very common term of respect. It is used in this way in the oral song above, '*Twon co*' (Our bull of men), as well as in Lawino's reference to Ocol's grandfather just quoted. The song to '*Mukumoi*', quoted below (p. 51), praises the great warrior as '*Twon dano pa abaa*' (Bull of men, son of my father). 'Son of the Bull' (p. 216) is one of the titles Lawino uses for Ocol in her final apostrophe to him, although elsewhere she questions his right to such a title when she asks 'Has the Bull died without a Head?' (p. 206). The 'Daughter of Lekamoi', Abul, is addressed as '*Nya pa twon*' (Daughter of the Bull), as is the leader of the girls in the Acoli dance that Lawino describes (*Wer pa Lawino*, p. 30; *Song of Lawino*, p. 34).

Because of its role in hunting and battle in achieving the manly reputation of a proud blower of horns and a bull among men, the spear is important as a practical object, a ritual object, and a symbol both of general manly qualities and specifically of sexual prowess and the penis. Spears occur frequently with little symbolic value in the battle accounts given in *otole* and *bwala* songs and in chiefdom *mwoc*, as in this *mwoc* of the Patiko chiefdom:

La-lak tongwa do,
Wan Patiko wacamo kalara
Warubu ki nyige;
Ee, eiya;
Morongole, eiya
Morongole, ee,
La-lak tongwa.

He is for the blades of our spears, oh;
We men of Patiko,

We eat hot pepper together with its seeds;
Ee, ee,
Morongole, ee,
He is for the blades of our spears.
(*Horn of My Love*, p. 174)[5]

The 'most popular and well known' *otole* song of a chiefdom is known as its 'spear song' ('Oral Literature Among the Acoli and Lang'o', p. 79). In this 'spear song' of the Atyak chiefdom, the spear mentioned, though still, in the context of an *otole* dance, a battle weapon, also expresses the idea of general fighting ability:

Tongnga romo iya,
Maya lwor;
Orobo tua camo nyikwara
Kom got;
. . .
Tonga romo iya,
Maya lwor.

I trust my spear,
The Maya are cowards;
Our men will earn battle honours
In the battle on the hill;
. . .
I trust my spear,
The Maya are cowards.
(*Horn of My Love*, p. 109)[6]

If a great warrior or hunter dies, his spears are placed on his grave all day and night (*Religion of the Central Luo*, p. 93); this funeral song for someone with the title '*Mukumoi*' (One who kills a man and a boy; *Horn of My Love*, p. 176) mourns the dead man through the idea of the neglected spears exposed to the cold and damp of night above the grave:

Mukumoi ye;
Twon dano pa aba;
Joni weko tong butu i koyo;
Joni oweko tong raa butu woko.
Tong raa nyal ocamo ye;
Kitino pa wora okwero an woko;
Mukumoi, oh,

Bull of men, son of my father;
The people have left the hippopotamus spear in the cold;
They have left the hippopotamus spear to sleep outside.
The hippopotamus spear has been eaten by rust;
The children of my father have rejected me;
(*Horn of My Love*, p. 128)

The ritual importance of the spear within the chiefdom system is explained by Taban lo Liyong at the beginning of his version of 'The Spear, Bead, and Bean Story':

> A man is not a man without his spear. With his spear he can defend his own and win his wars and kill his game. In our spear, our manhood resides. In our manhood, our spears are found. A chief has his drums of rule. He must also have the royal spear in which the collective might of his people resides. If he loses this spear the kingdom falls.
> (Taban lo Liyong, *Eating Chiefs*, p. 3)

This myth, which is known in outline to all Luo groups, inculcates the idea of chiefly power depending on continued possession of the royal spear. It concerns the grandsons of the first man, Luo, the Chief Labongo and his brother Kipir (or Gipir). The main incident begins with an elephant's invasion of their farm:

Cong mo lyec obino ka camo poto
Kipir otingo tong ocobo ki lyec
Lyec ocito woko ki tong.
Tong onongo pa Labongo,
Labongo okeco matek
Odido ominne pi tong.
Kikelle tong mukere, Labongo degi;
Kikelle dyel, Labongo degi;
Kikelle dyang, Labongo degi,

One day the elephant came to eat the field
Kipir took a spear and speared the elephant with it
The elephant went away with the spear.
The spear was Labongo's spear,
Labongo, he was angry very strongly
He pested his brother for the spear.
They brought him another spear, Labongo refused;
They brought him a goat, Labongo refused;

They brought him a cow, Labongo refused;
('Oral Literature Among the Acoli and Lang'o', pp. 44–7)

Kipir was forced to trail the elephant in search of the lost spear and after a long and difficult journey came to the house of '*Min Lyec*' (The mother of elephants) who had the spear and was persuaded to let Kipir take it. She gave Kipir food for the return journey and some very rare beads. Labongo got his spear back and there was peace between the brothers until a child of Labongo's accidentally swallowed one of Kipir's rare beads. Kipir was as implacable over the return of his rare bead as Labongo had been for the return of his spear and Labongo eventually capitulated and slit open his baby son's[7] belly to get back the bead. Thereafter the brothers and their families parted and (it is implied) the great divisions and migrations amongst Luo peoples began (loc. cit.).

In his account of the ceremonies at the ancestral shrine in *Religion of the Central Luo*, Okot indicates the ritual importance of the spear within the clan group. The shrine was an untidily built miniature hut (*ot jok*) which was the 'house' of the ancestors and an *okango* shrub was planted next to it. In the central part of the dedication of the shrine, the *okango* was used as a spear rest for a bunch of spears tied together which represented 'not only the might of the Pa-Cua in battle, but also the hunting and sexual prowess of the young men'. The chant of prayers at the shrine followed and thereafter the leaders of the ceremony took the bundle of spears and danced *bwola* dance steps from the shrine and into a hut, whilst a woman poured water on to the roof of the hut above the entrance, wetting both the spears and the young men. Okot comments on the laughter of the women, their pleasure in the pouring of the water, and the ambivalence of symbolic meaning of the spears:

> . . . whereas the old men took the spear to represent the might of the clan and the hunting prowess of their hunters, the young women were joking with the young men about sex. The spear was taken as the symbol of manhood, representing the penis. Thus the women pouring water on the roof and wetting the young men was represented as 'cooling' the virility of the men.
> (*Religion of the Central Luo*, pp. 98–101; cf. *Song of Lawino*, p. 158)

In the next song, a spirit possession song, Okot suggests that the sexual meaning of the spear is the only meaning. It is one of a group of songs sung during spirit possession ceremonies which were not associated with a particular form of *jok* but with the sexual privileges that the diviner had when he came to perform his ceremonies in a particular homestead. The exact nature of these privileges is not made clear ('Oral Literature Among the Acoli and

Lang'o', p. 277). As translated in *Horn of My Love*, the song is a prayer for increased manly potency:

Tong ma lake tek,
Kako lela;
Tong ma yam ageno,
Baro lela;
Ladwar obutu i tim;
Ato woko;
Tong ma yam ageno,
Kako lela;
Tong ma lake bit,
Cubu lela;

The spear with the hard point,
Let it split the granite rock;
The spear that I trust,
Let it split the granite rock;
The hunter has slept in the wilderness,
I am dying, oh;
The spear that I trust,
Let it split the granite rock;
The spear with the sharp point,
Let it crack the granite rock;
(*Horn of My Love*, p. 91)

Okot explains that the 'penis of the man in this song is likened to a hard-headed spear penetrating into a hard rock. The woman, perhaps unwilling, keeps her thighs tightly closed' ('Oral Literature Among the Acoli and Lang'o', p. 281). Certain phrases used in this song, and particularly '*Tong ma yam ageno*' (The spear that I trust), frequently occur in many different types of oral song[8]. The symbolic value of the spear in Acoli literature and society is wide-ranging and complex; in his work on Acoli literature and religion, Okot is particularly concerned to emphasize its sexual connotations.

As Lawino's 'Song' is little concerned with hunting or war, spears are mentioned as weapons on only one occasion (*Wer pa Lawino*, p. 115; *Song of Lawino*, p. 169), but on a few occasions they are used with a specifically sexual reference which is usually underlined deliberately in the English version. The boys forcibly separated from girls in missionary boarding schools are described as being '*calo i-pala ma kili*' (p. 89), 'like knives / Without handles' (p. 124) but the English version alone continues with an echo of the funeral song of the warrior '*Mukumoi*' (see above, p. 51):

And the spears
Of the lone hunters,
The trusted right-hand spears
Of young bulls
Rust in the dewy cold
Of the night. (p. 124)

In Section 10, when Lawino explains the reaction of the clan to misfortunes that involve the whole community, both versions include references to prayers that the young men's 'trusted spears', '*Tong ma lugeno*', should stay 'sharp', '*bit*' and should not be left out 'In the dewy cold' (p. 171) '*bong' kupot toyo*' (p. 116). In *Wer pa Lawino* a song similar to the spirit possession song '*Tong ma lake tek*, 'The spear with the hard point', is quoted to reinforce these ideas, whilst in the English version Lawino prays that the young men's spears:

. . . should strike the death spot
Deep and painful!
Then the young cobs
Will scream
And shed tears of sweet pains! (p. 171)

Ocol's spiritual cure at the end of the poem is dependent on the blessing of the elders. In *Wer pa Lawino*, Ocol is told to '*Bak dogi botgi, leg tong' gucommi*,' (p. 145; Apologize to them, ask them to make you a spear); in *Song of Lawino* there is an extensive echo from the spirit possession song '*Tong ma lake tek*' (The spear that I trust), and this once again ends in an emphasis which underlines the sexual symbolism of the spear, as Lawino compares Ocol's old, soft spear to 'an earth-worm' and says she is 'sick / Of sharing a bed with a woman' (p. 213). Okot considers the sexual implications of the spear to be of very great importance and modifies his translation to make sure that they are underlined in the English version.

Inevitably, there have been some losses of idiomatic and proverbial meaning through translation. In the second section, Lawino reports Ocol's rejection of the idea of living with someone like her 'Who has not been to school', but in the Acoli version only she says his words are '*ming'u pa "ikucu-buru*"' (p. 23; the stupidity of the 'playing in ashes' age group—cf. *Song of Lawino*, p. 27); in other words she accuses him of childishness in an oblique way. Similarly, the beginning of the section on dances contains a reference to sand for cleaning teeth as a token of love that was discussed in relation to the oral song '*Kel kweyo*' (see above, p. 21) which has been left out of the translation:

'*Lak tar, nong'o lujwayo ki kweyo*' (p. 28; they have white teeth, they cleaned them with sand). Lawino's description of the low status of bachelors is supported by her use of the proverb '*Labot kilwango ka dek wi kot*' ('Oral Literature Among the Acoli and Lang'o', p. 335; the unmarried young man is called to a meal in the rain). Both versions describe a 'bald' and 'toothless' old unmarried man, but where *Wer pa Lawino* summarizes his low status by referring to that proverb '*pud lulwong'i ka dek la-wi-kot*' (p. 78; you are still invited to a meal in the rain), *Song of Lawino* contains only the lines 'if you are unmarried / You are nothing' (p. 105). In all of these cases, and a few others, Okot has dealt with a difficulty in the translation in the simplest way by leaving out the obscurity which caused the difficulty. This kind of problem may be part of the reason for the omission of Section 14 from the English poem, as the section is full of proverbial sayings. In addition to the constant reference to the proverb of the pumpkin, the second and third of the passages quoted from the section above (pp. 39–40) illustrate the density of other proverbs within the section.

Occasionally Okot's literal translation produces other curious obscurities, for example the comparison of Clementine's mouth to 'the mouth of a fiend' (p. 22) which is meaningless in English. There is often obscurity in unexplained references to social customs, for example the reference of Lawino to Ocol's brother as her 'husband-in-law', which is separate from her later explanation of the fact that a brother inherits a wife along with other property (pp. 183 and 185) or to religious beliefs, as in the unexplained reference to 'The kite with the flame / In its anus' (p. 153) or the very briefly explained examples of 'free *jok*', the spirits that possess people and cause diseases (p. 157). All of these examples are illustrations of a degree of lost meaning consequent upon the translation of *Wer pa Lawino*, some of which might have been avoided by a different kind of translation.

The superficial virtue of this method of translation is its exotic aspect: what may be proverbial or even cliché in Acoli, through literal translation becomes vivid and original and provokes new insights in a new language. Okot is clearly aware of these possibilities as he occasionally makes use of unnaturally literal translation. He talks, for example, of the number of weeks 'In four moons' (p. 85) instead of four months, and he retains the Acoli words for 'eating' (p. 129) Acoli praise names, when the natural translation would use 'to win' or 'to be given'. In relation to Christian names he retains the phrase 'to buy a name' (p. 114) in the passage where he is concerned with training for baptism, to translate '*willo nying*'' (p. 84), but translates '*mako nying*'' (p. 12; to catch a name) in the more natural way as 'baptized' or 'christened' (p. 14). The most obvious and striking example of this is his retranslation of missionaries' mistranslations of the vocabulary of Christian belief, behind which lies the history of the blunders of the missionaries in their first dealings with the Acoli at the beginning of this century. In *African Religions in Western Scholarship*, Okot records one of the explanations later missionaries have given of how the word *Rubanga* came to be used among the Acoli as a name for the Christian God:

> In 1911, Italian Catholic priests put before a group of Acoli elders the question 'Who created you?'; and because the Luo language does not have an independent concept of *create* or *creation*, the question was rendered to mean, 'Who moulded you?'. But this was still meaningless, because human beings are born of their mothers. The elders told the visitors that they did not know. But, we are told that this reply was unsatisfactory, and the missionaries insisted that a satisfactory answer must be given. One of the elders remembered that, although a person may be born normally, when he is afflicted with tuberculosis of the spine, then he loses his normal figure, he gets 'moulded'. So he said '*Rubanga* is the one who moulds people'. This is the name of the hostile spirit which the Acoli believe causes the hunch or hump on the back.
> [Okot p'Bitek, *African Religions in Western Scholarship*, p. 62.]

To keep this idea alive, Okot refers to 'the good word', 'the clean book', 'the clean ghost', 'skyland', and 'the Hunchback', which are deliberately odd translations giving a totally new effect in the translation from that given in the original, where the Christian meanings of the words would be accepted without any strangeness by now.

This aspect of Okot's translation particularly irritated Taban lo Liyong. He says that although to Okot 'the Catholic translation of catechism into Acoli . . . is poor . . . Okot's own translation of that catechism into his Acoli-English . . . is no nearer to the original English or Latin or Greek or Acoli' (Taban lo Liyong, *The Last Word*, p. 140). Whether or not Okot has totally escaped from the old battles with Catholics that might be one result of his Protestant upbringing, his essential point in his use of 'Acoli-English' in matters relating to religion is a serious one. He believes that the missionaries could not find suitable translations for their concepts because the concepts themselves were alien to Acoli religious tradition, a view to which he has converted at least one bishop,[9] albeit an Anglican one. He is not simply using exotic language for its own sake. Taban lo Liyong is critical also of Okot's translation method throughout the poem:

> . . . the meaning of deep Acoli proverbs are made very, very light by their rendition into English *word for word*, rather than *sense for sense* or *proverb for proverb*. So Okot has devalued Acoli *gagi* for a trifle English ten cents. . . .
> (*The Last Word*, p. 141)

He is partially concerned with the loss of meaning that we have noted and partially concerned with the devaluation of a proverbial literature involved in the quotation of proverbs whose proverbial nature is not clear in the translation. On both counts his criticism has considerable validity, but the alternative he suggests of translation 'proverb for proverb' would have been disastrous as it would have meant the abandonment of that use of verbal elements in oral literature which was present in *Wer pa Lawino*.

Okot's dependence on oral tradition in terms of form and verbal details is one of the ways in which he attempts to deal with the dilemma of a Westernized élite writing for and about a much less Westernized African society. His submission to oral tradition in literature parallels the submission to the 'real masters' of African philosophy in the villages that he recommends in his essays. A translation 'proverb for proverb' would have made him, in the English version only, an 'interpreter' of Lawino when he was seeking only to 'describe' her (see 'African Religions in an African University', in *Africa's Cultural Revolution*, pp. 85–93).[10] The few examples of unnaturally literal translation are similar to those other aspects of Lawino that make her a little out of date, and therefore 'a complete outsider' in relation to Westernization, that are discussed below (pp. 72 and 119) in the context of her characterization. The feeling of the authenticity of Lawino's voice, both as the 'voice of the peasantry' (see below, pp. 102 ff.) and as a 'real master' of things African (see below, p. 152) is conveyed by Okot's use of the aspects of oral literature that we have looked at and he chose the only method of translation that would enable him to retain these features which are vital to the success of the English poem.

Notes to Chapter 4

1. All these proverbs appear in 'Oral Literature Among the Acoli and Lang'o' and their meaning is discussed. see pp. 317–80.
2. Line 5 is literally 'you saw the son of Alal', see also the funeral song quoted below, p. 85.
3. Literally: 'Horns and trumpets are everywhere.'
4. Literally: 'But in the past, the name of our homestead used to blow.' In this quotation and the previous one, the Acoli does not mention the horn, but the use of '*kutu*' (blows) implies it.
5. See pp. 102, 104, 113 and 164. *Mwoc* means nickname; the *mwoc* of a chiefdom expresses the pride of its members and will be shouted out in whole or in part in battle, in *otole* dances, and on less formal occasions when members of different chiefdoms meet.
6. '*Tong roma iya*' is literally: 'My spear satisfies my insides.'
7. 'Daughter' in some accounts; cf. Taban lo Liyong, *Eating Chiefs*, p. 5.

8. For example: *Religion of the Central Luo*, p. 101; Cliff Lubwa p'Chong, 'Vernacular Themes in Our Schools', p. 1.
9. See J. K. Russell, *Men Without God*?, London: The Highway Press, 1966, especially pp. 6 and 82. Russell acknowledges 'the generous and unfailing help' of Okot in writing the book in his Preface and draws substantially on Okot's descriptions of Acoli religious practices.
10. This essay is discussed below, pp. 131 and 134.

5 Characterization

IN *Anatomy of Criticism*, Northrop Frye distinguishes between 'fictional' and 'thematic' aspects of literature. The fictional aspect is the 'internal fiction' of plot and the relationship 'of the hero and his society' and the thematic aspect is the writer's idea or ideas and depends on the 'external fiction' of 'a relation between the writer and the writer's society'. A reader who is anxious to know how a story will end is concerned with the fictional aspect of a work, whilst the reader who asks about the 'point' of a story is concerned with its thematic aspect. Frye says that this distinction can be applied to all literature. Even the kind of narrative where the writer tells the story without making any comment whatever on the action has a thematic aspect to it; we can discuss the ideas that lie behind the story and the ways in which the story implies a comment in the writer's own society. Similarly, even works where the writer seems to talk to the reader directly and openly express his own ideas or personality contain a fictional aspect because in these works the writer dramatizes himself and his relationship with the reader. All works therefore contain both fictional and thematic elements, and 'the question of which is more important is often simply a matter of opinion or emphasis in interpretation' (Northrop Frye, *Anatomy of Criticism: Four Essays*, pp. 52–3).

The paradox of a dramatic monologue is that it lacks overt narrative structure; it has no plot, the basic outline of most fictional works. Yet the writer assumes the voice of a fictional personality and totally eliminates his own voice. The assumed voice is used partly as a way of expressing the poet's own attitudes directly to the reader, but is also to some extent an independent fictional entity. Problems of interpretation of such poems may relate to a misunderstanding of the ways in which the fictional personality is acting as a mask or mouthpiece for the poet. Critics of Okot's 'Songs' sometimes appear to assume that the singers are nothing other than mouthpieces for Okot and attempt to identify the points of view of the singers with those of Okot. In his essay 'Okot p'Bitek: Writer, Singer or Culturizer', Maina Gathungu illustrates the problems that arise because of this approach when he tries, as he puts it, 'to "fix" Okot in the literary field' by working out Okot's attitudes to his own 'Singers' using biographical information as well as the internal evidence of the poems. Of *Song of Lawino*, we are told that Lawino is 'living . . . persuasive and truly convincing', whilst Ocol is 'hopelessly on the defensive' and this leads the critic to conclude that 'Okot is here trying to identify himself with the traditional forces'. When he discusses *Song of Ocol* and *Song of Lawino* together, he changes the identification:

> If in *Song of Lawino* one identifies Okot with Ocol (whose description he would seem to fit), one feels that Okot has miserably failed to justify his education, adoption of new ways, weakness of the old and the extent of his adoption. Lawino—representing the old in its entirety—comes out victorious. Okot's essays on these grounds founder as it were and rather paradoxically his work soars above his personality.
> (Maina Gathungu, 'Okot p'Bitek: Writer, Singer or Culturizer', in Chris L. Wanjala (ed.), *Standpoints on African Literature*, pp. 52–5)

The hidden first axiom of this essay is that the poet must be identified with one or both of the singers and cannot be detached from both. At the end of his essay on 'Song of Prisoner', another critic, Atieno Odhiambo, appears to identify Okot with the prisoner in a similar way:

> The writer must know how to penetrate the working and peasant masses and how to turn bourgeois-structure inconveniences . . . into revolutionary situations. The prisoner must not go out to dance and forget. The intellectual must help the masses to rise out of the enveloping despair that comes with the expansion of the petty-bourgeois class. . . .
> (ibid., p. 112)

This paragraph gives three names to the voice we hear in 'Song of Prisoner', 'the writer', 'the prisoner' and 'the intellectual'; Atieno Odhiambo is assuming that the poet's ideas must be directly expressed by the words of the singer, the prisoner.

Margaret Marshment, in her reply to Atieno Odhiambo's essay, treats 'Song of Prisoner', in contrast, as fictional in the manner of drama. She begins by illustrating and criticizing Odhiambo's identification of Okot with the prisoner, and goes on to explain:

> All Okot's 'songs' are dramatic poems—each is sung by a character created by the poet. Lawino, Ocol, Malaya, the Prisoner are not 'masks' or 'personae' for the poet: they are 'characters' as much as characters in a play are; and they should be approached as such; they should not be identified with the poet: opinions expressed by the characters in the poems should never be extracted and presented as the views of Okot—at least not without careful consideration of the context of the 'Singer' and his or her situation.
> (ibid., p. 127)

She discusses the 'internal fiction' of the poem, the problems that caused the prisoner's arrest, and the nature of his reaction to the pressures of society on him, asserting that both writer and reader are detached from the prisoner and view him with a mixture 'of compassion and criticism'. She says that 'the irony arising from the gap between the vision of the Prisoner and our vision of the Prisoner's vision is the meaning of the poem' (loc. cit.). The idea of all the poems as dramatic poems is examined in this chapter and the next two chapters. Though each poem, except 'Song of Malaya', has a substantial 'internal fiction', only Lawino of the singers is a consistent and plausible individual characterization. Each singer, except the malaya, represents the dilemma of a particular social group in East Africa and especially in Acoliland. Chapter 6 discusses the relationship of Okot's mode of characterization and his techniques as a satirist and those of oral composers and Chapter 7 illustrates Okot's success in using his singers to represent different groups in conflict in East African society. The final chapter concentrates chiefly on the ways in which the singers can be seen as mouthpieces, expressing Okot's ideas directly to the non-fictional writer's audience.

One difficulty in discussing the fictions of Okot's 'Songs' is that all of them, except 'Song of Prisoner', have a thematic structure. Sections 1 and 2 of *Song of Lawino* introduce us briefly to the fictional situation in the poem, but then Lawino deals with one particular aspect of Western influence on Acoli tradition in each of the other sections. The early sections deal with concrete things; dances, ornaments and games, hair styles, and cooking, whilst the later sections deal with more abstract subjects: time, missionary education, Christian myths, medicine, and politics. Sections 12 and 13 conclude the argument, tying the themes together in their extended metaphors. Ocol dismisses Lawino's argument with a succession of contemptuous smiles and is then free to follow his own thematic outline. He begins with a generalized condemnation of the 'Blackness' (p. 19) of Africa, including his own blackness and follows this with a vigorous summary of the measures to be taken to destroy all images of 'The blackness of the past' (p. 31). He moves to particular issues, mocking the traditional treatment of African women, the hopeless impoverishment of pastoral communities, and the murmurings of political dissent from the poor. Lawino's clansmen appear for the concluding movement of the poem, where they are urged to say their nostalgic farewells to the village and march into the city from which, Ocol reminds us, nearly all images of the black past have been eradicated. 'Song of Malaya' begins with a summary demonstration of society's need for prostitutes and ends with a summary of society's expressions of contempt for prostitutes. The sections in between each reflect one aspect of society's ambivalence towards prostitution.

There is no thematic structure in 'Song of Prisoner'. It is also different from the other poems in its very specific and pervasive sense of the prisoner's present situation. Unlike the other 'singers', the prisoner begins by telling us where he is: he is lying in the 'powerful arms' of 'the stone floor' surrounded by 'bleak white walls' (pp. 11–12). In addition to the severe discomforts of that position, he is suffering the effects of a recent and thorough beating-up (p. 14). He can also hear, in his imagination or from just outside his cell, 'the hollow laughs' of his 'uniformed Brothers', the warders who have just beaten him (p. 16). Throughout the poem we are frequently reminded of the bareness of his prison and the fact that he is still there, and much of the poetry in the first five sections contains more description of his physical suffering. Later, the sense of physical suffering decreases as the poem comes to be dominated by delusions of release. But we are repeatedly reminded that we are still in the prison either by the 'rope' that is binding the prisoner's limbs (p. 102) or by the 'steel door' or 'steel gate' of the cell.

Because there is no description of their immediate surroundings from the other singers, there is no similar sense of time and place in the other songs; the singers' situations can only be guessed at through the apostrophe they use. Lawino may be assumed to be singing to herself alone, she may be singing to her husband, or in a public place to her clansmen and her husband together. The song may be sung in one place at one time or there might be a time lag in the course of the song. Ocol appears to start in the home from which he is ejecting Lawino, to have moved to the market place for his political self-defence, and to have transferred himself to the capital when he addresses the dignitaries of the nation at the end of the poem. The first three sections of 'Song of Malaya' create a sense of a specific time of day for the poem: the beginning of the whore's night's work. The men pouring out of their prisons, ships, and work places converge on the whorehouses in Section 1 and after this the prostitutes are urged to prepare for them, first to 'Go gay and clean' (p. 133), next to 'go out into the open World' to pick up the men (p. 142), and then to 'Bear these wretches / Into your heaven' (p. 154). This progression from the beginning of their preparations to the climax of their activities holds the beginning of the poem together but the attack on the bishop makes the poem more abstract and the appeal to prostitutes throughout Uganda and the mention of those harlots who are famous in Christian history (pp. 163–7) completely destroys the impression of a specific evening implied by the beginning of the poem.

Apostrophe also contributes in an imprecise way to our understanding of another aspect of the singers' immediate situation, the possible existence of a fictional audience for their song. Whilst the sense of fictional audience often fades for parts of the 'Songs', it contributes to the dramatic force of parts of each poem. In *Song of Lawino* the only situation in which Lawino could, with dramatic credibility, address herself to her husband and clansmen in the same time and place would be if she were appealing to her clansmen to intervene in her marriage dispute. The juxtaposition of the appeals to Ocol and the clansmen and the nature of her appeal to the clansmen in Section 1 suggest just this situation. The first thirty-three lines of the poem are addressed to Ocol and then Lawino appears to break off from her argument to appeal for the community's sympathy in her wrestling with the injustices that Ocol has heaped on her:

> My clansmen, I cry
> Listen to my voice:
> The insults of my man
> Are painful beyond bearing. (p. 15)

It sounds very much like an appeal for help. It appears that Lawino has not found Ocol amenable to reason within the privacy of the cooking hut, and is taking her dispute into the centre of the compound and asking the community to intervene on her behalf. This implied situation is partially marred by the way in which her tone changes from that defensive appeal through mockery to the serenely patronizing tone with which the poem ends. We also lose sight of it altogether in those sections where no apostrophe is used; in these, the fictional emphasis shifts to certain experiences in her past and the 'external fiction' of Lawino's direct relationship with the reader replaces the situation implied by the apostrophe. The idea of the clansmen as arbiters is revived when she appeals to them in Section 12 (pp. 199 and 207), but only very briefly. Their presence as fictional hearers provides an occasional extra dimension to the poem rather than a consistent dramatic situation.

In *Song of Ocol*, only Lawino is addressed in more than one section, although many different groups of people are addressed, and therefore the idea of a fictional audience is totally confused. At the beginning of the poem, Lawino is apparently thrown out of Ocol's house and near the end Ocol sees her 'Under the tree' (p. 80), weeping; these two events suggest a possible outline for the whole poem of Ocol chasing Lawino out of his house and continuing to harangue her in front of a growing gathering of astonished clansmen. This outline gains some support from the overheard whisper of Ocol's constituent (p. 55) and the mutterings of the beggar (p. 65). Section 6 exploits the sense of a fictional audience in a sustained manner by the comparisons Ocol makes between the labour of his education and the carefree activities of the whisperer. Ocol takes his challenger on an imaginary tour of his properties to prepare for the question as to whether he expected to find gold 'Along the village pathways' (p. 62) as a result of Uhuru. Elsewhere in the poem, there is no sense of a fictional audience and most of Ocol's harangue is directed over the heads of the clansmen. The only conceivable fictional audience for the malaya's 'Song' is the group of fellow prostitutes whom she addresses at the end of nearly every section (pp. 132, 141, 154, 163, 174 and 184). Unlike those addressed by the other 'singers', they are in agreement with the malaya and are therefore totally passive; their actions or words are never reported. Their presence provides a motive for the malaya in singing her 'Song', that of the encouragement of her comrades despite the difficulties they face. In 'Song of Prisoner' the fictional audience is the group of warders who are mentioned in six of the sections (pp. 14, 68, 75, 82, 102 and 116) so that their presence is felt by the reader throughout the poem. The prisoner makes their unresponsiveness clear, calling them 'uniformed Brothers', 'deaf Brother' and 'uniformed Stone' and this makes them seem more like furniture of imprisonment than a human audience between the prisoner and the reader. The mention of the judge (p. 16), and the reiteration of the judge's question, further extend the internal fiction by suggesting either that the prisoner is awaiting trial or that he has appeared in court and been remanded to appear again. He tells us that he has not yet pleaded or been found guilty (p. 16).

Song of Lawino and *Song of Ocol* rapidly evoke a fictional outline because of the conventional nature of the situation from which they arise: the dilemma of the Westernized man, ill at ease with village culture and in confrontation with those who have not travelled, is both socially commonplace and an established literary convention in African literatures in European languages. For a readership minimally aware of African literature or society, Section 1 of *Song of Lawino*, despite the paucity of information it gives, implies a clear fictional outline. Okot then complicates matters by introducing the universal social commonplace and literary convention of the eternal triangle of the jealousies aroused by the relationships of one man and two women. *Song of Ocol* arises out of the same conventional conflicts but does not exploit them because Ocol directs our eyes elsewhere. Background information is never allowed to interrupt the thematic format of *Song of Lawino, Song of Ocol*, or 'Song of Malaya'. It is never introduced primarily to explain the singer's predicament, but only emerges when it is used as evidence in argument. For example, in *Song of Lawino*, having told us how Ocol now treats her, Lawino tells us at the beginning of Section 2 that 'only recently' they were very close to each other (p. 21) but she does not explain in any way why this change might have taken place. It is not until much later that we are told, in passing, that Ocol has been 'in the white man's country' (p. 66) and it is even later before we find out that he 'has read at Makerere University' (p. 140). In the circumstances, it seems reasonable to guess that the time away from home helped to cause Ocol's change of attitude, but Lawino certainly makes no attempt to make it clear.

Out of Lawino's anecdotes throughout *Song of Lawino*, a coherent, if not detailed, picture of Lawino, Ocol, and the history of their relationship emerges. Lawino's liveliness and beauty earned her the admiration of many young men, including Ocol, and therefore the honorary title 'chief of girls' (p. 43). She had very little indeed to do with the missionaries, although her older sister became a Protestant and Lawino had the chance of becoming a Christian. Ocol was apparently a convert at a fairly young age, and therefore received a thorough mission schooling, but still wooed Lawino enthusiastically and eventually they married. At first they were happy, but then Ocol went to the university and the 'white man's country' and returned transformed in status and life style, totally unable to reconcile himself to Lawino's modes of behaviour and finding the Westernized Clementine much more attractive. Although in its introduction and conclusion *Song of Ocol* depends on the fiction of the relationship between Ocol and Lawino, little use is made of it and nothing added to it. Ocol's interest in local or domestic issues is very slight. He never mentions Clementine and disposes of the other half of his problem by throwing Lawino out of his house (p. 9). Because he is concerned with public matters, the pursuit of his argument does not lead to the use of information from his past as evidence.

It is an indication of something in Okot's attitude to the singers in *Two Songs* that neither is given a proper name. Even the definite article 'the' malaya or 'the' prisoner which are most commonly used in discussions of the poems are the critics' own addition. In the East African Publishing House edition of *Two Songs*, neither title contains an article; they are: 'Song of Prisoner' and 'Song of Malaya'. In the African edition which contains 'Song of Prisoner' alone, it is called *Song of a Prisoner*. The lack of a proper name in itself weakens the internal fiction of the poems and the omission of the article suggests that the characters are types of the categories 'prisoner' and 'prostitute',[1] rather than individuals. The internal fiction of 'Song of Malaya' is virtually non-existent and certainly not adequate to support characterization, as the most superficial comparison of the poem with Okello Oculi's *Prostitute* indicates. The malaya is the only one of Okot's singers who is not clearly an Acoli; more significantly, we do not know where she is from, even in the more general terms of whether she has urban or peasant origins, or how she became a prostitute. In contrast, Oculi's description of the village's sacrifice of Rosa to the pleasures of the visiting minister occupies most of his first chapter (Okello Oculi, *Prostitute*, pp. 11–21). All that we learn of the malaya's past, information that comes, as in *Song of Lawino*, near the end of the poem, is that she has two children (pp. 169–71), and a married brother who has disowned her (p. 175). Again the contrast with Rosa's account of her friend Rebecca and of the 'mulatto' (ibid., pp. 102–32) is very pronounced.

Another difficulty in viewing *Song of Lawino* and *Song of Ocol* as predominantly fiction relates to the consistency and plausibility of the characters. Northrop Frye sees 'the tendency to verisimilitude', the plausible representation of experience and especially of human character, as 'one of the two poles of literature' (*Anatomy of Criticism*, p. 51). A description of the extent to which the characters are plausible is therefore a good way of defining the nature of the internal fiction of the 'Songs'. In his review of *Wer pa Lawino*, Okumo pa' Lukobo suggests that there is a contradiction between the two conventional situations in the poem: the clash of values and the eternal triangle.

> In choosing as his text: '*Te okono bong' luputu*' (Don't uproot the pumpkin) I think p'Bitek has made a mistake. What Lawino has to say would have been better expressed by another Acoli proverb which says '*Dako abila ni aye meni*' (Your first wife is your mother). For what Lawino is really concerned with is a personal matter—her rivalry with her husband's mistress Kelementina.
> (Okumo pa'Lukobo, review of *Wer pa Lawino*, in *Nanga*)

Okumo pa'Lukobo thinks that the contradiction can only be reconciled by treating the clash of values as nothing more than an expression of Lawino's jealousy of Clementine:

> Lawino knows very well that the homely pumpkin she defends cannot compare with the succulent grapes which—like the fox in the fable—she cannot reach and so calls 'sour' . . . Lawino, burning with rage and jealousy, pretends to despise what she cannot have herself.
> (loc. cit.)

He quotes from Lawino's tirade against cosmetics in Section 2 to illustrate the extravagance of her 'vituperation' (loc. cit.) of Clementine. Here, Lawino is at her most mercurial. She begins Section 2 with nostalgia, recalling the time when she was happy with Ocol and 'used to admire him speaking in English' (p. 22). Then she abuses Clementine and mocks her use of cosmetics. At the peak of her abuse, she abruptly changes pace:

> Forgive me, brother,
> Do not think I am insulting
> The woman with whom I share my husband!
> Do not think my tongue
> Is being sharpened by jealousy.
> It is the sight of Tina
> That provokes sympathy from my heart. (p. 24)

Having denied that jealousy has prompted her, she immediately confesses that, nevertheless, she may be 'a little jealous':

I do not deny
I am a little jealous.
It is no good lying,
We all suffer from a little jealousy.
It catches you unawares
Like the ghosts that bring fevers; (p. 24)

At this point the 'internal fiction' in the poem is as strong as it ever is, because the reader is made to overhear Lawino in confrontation with three other fictional performers, Ocol, Clementine, and the 'brother' whom for those two paragraphs she is addressing. The violent changes of mood in the whole section direct the reader's attention away from what she is saying to the nature of such an unstable speaker and this particular passage is good dramatic verse in that her change of mind about her jealousy seems to suggest that the confession she makes has been wrung from her, perhaps by the sceptical face of the 'brother', and her insistence that jealousy 'catches you unawares' implies that she is genuinely struggling to understand her own emotions.

She falters only momentarily into this possible show of weakness before returning to the counterattack by reasserting that 'pity' rather than jealousy is the emotion Clementine rouses in her (p. 25). At this point most readers surely agree with Okumo pa'Lukubo in feeling a little sceptical about the genuineness of Lawino's pity, especially as she immediately goes on to compare Clementine's breasts with 'bits of cow-hide' and a few lines later accuses her of having had many abortions (p. 25). Nevertheless his view of Lawino's character is not consistent with the facts of the whole poem. In later sections it is made clear on a number of occasions that Lawino has been offered and has rejected many of the 'succulent grapes' that Clementine enjoys. She implies that she has had the chance to dance the ballroom dance (p. 41); her description of 'White men's cooking stoves' (pp. 66–9) suggest that she has tried to use them and later we learn that Ocol has left 'a large clock' in her care (p. 86). Her description of the Protestant service and the Catholic Evening Speaker's Class (pp. 113–20) make it clear that Lawino had the opportunity for conversion and thus education. 'Sour grapes' may seem a possible explanation of Lawino's attack on Clementine in the context of Section 2 alone, but it raises many contradictions if we consider the whole poem.

Her jealousy of Clementine can be seen in a slightly different light so as to reinforce her championship of Acoli culture rather than to contradict it. Sections 3 to 6, like Section 2, are concerned to a great extent with Lawino's rivalry with Clementine.[2] These same sections create the impression of Lawino's pride in her own beauty and womanly accomplishments within the traditional mores of Acoli society and it is the juxtaposition of these two kinds of description which provides the key to the nature of the rivalry between the two women. Lawino does feel 'pity' for Clementine and her kind in their failure to match her in her accomplishments at the *orak* dance as chief of youths (p. 32), when walking to the well with her hair adorned (pp. 56–7), or as she works at the grinding stone with her sister (p. 74). Her jealousy of Clementine is aggravated beyond measure because she does not understand how Ocol can find Clementine attractive. Lawino's 'rantings about culture' which Okumu pa'Lukobo dismissed so readily (op. cit.) are inextricably involved in her rivalry with Clementine.

Lawino's jealousy is not that of a wife who expects sole possession of her husband as of right; she knows no other kind of marriage than polygamy and understands that rivalry is almost certain to arise between co-wives. A few lines after her confession of 'a little jealousy' she insists that she does not want sole possession of Ocol:

> I am not unfair to my husband,
> I do not complain
> Because he wants another woman
> Whether she is young or aged!
> Who has ever prevented men
> From wanting women? (p. 27)

Polygamous marriage as an institution accommodates the true nature of sexual appetites and the wise wife in the polygamous household is quite able to handle her co-wives; only the foolish become jealous:

> When I have another woman
> With whom I share my husband,
> I am glad
> A woman who is jealous
> Of another, with whom she shares a man,
> Is jealous because she is slow,
> Lazy and shy,
> Because she is cold, weak, clumsy! (p. 28)

As a former 'chief of girls' Lawino is sure she can compete with any woman. She knows she was attractive and is attractive still, she twice tells us that her skin is still smooth (pp. 43 and 63) and she has a boyfriend who even now praises its smoothness. The hazy figure of Clementine is an excellent foil for Lawino, despite Okot's shadowy portrait of her. Clementine is a Westernized girl who straightens her hair and uses cosmetics and is perhaps a little past her prime. Clementine's age is the most worrying fact about her in Lawino's mind, since a first wife can expect her husband to be attracted by rivals who have the bloom of youth on their side, but not by her own age-mates and certainly not by this 'age-mate of my mother' (p. 26). Clementine must have deceived Ocol about her age by the tricks that modern girls use:

> How aged modern women
> Pretend to be young girls! (p. 25)

The remarks about breasts and abortion which follow underline the implication that Clementine is older than she pretends to be.

The later sections contain only one reference to Clementine, and are certainly not primarily concerned with womanly rivalry, but Lawino's womanly pride is often involved in her response to Ocol. It was the sound of her song, her praises on the lips of the young men floating into the cold hall of the Evening Speakers' Class from the get-stuck dance, that persuaded Lawino to walk out in the middle of the class (pp. 118–19) and her pride in her own attractions that made her so indignant about the ugly teacher's advances (p. 125). In Section 9, she tells us she is 'not a shy woman' (p. 142) and will not be bullied into silence by those who refuse to answer her questions. At the very end of the poem, her rivalry with Clementine makes a brief reappearance when she mentions again 'the woman / With whom I share you' and begs Ocol to give her 'one more chance' to show him 'The wealth in your house' (pp 215–16). In the early sections, her tongue is sharpened by the pangs of offended vanity, and repeatedly throughout the poem her most urgent appeal to Ocol is to 'stop the insults' (p. 29) which cut into her very identity, her womanly pride.

Intertwined with this vanity amongst her age-mates is Lawino's pride in her family and respect for the standards of family life, standards which Ocol repeatedly tramples on with his new ideas. The climax of her description of her youthful beauty is the respect it won her from her brothers:

> . . . my brothers called me *Nya-Dyang*
> For my breasts shook
> And beckoned the cattle . . . (p. 44)

She goes on from this to describe the beauty of her old house where Ocol came to woo her. Later in the poem, she lovingly describes the inside of her mother's house, beginning with her father's 'revered stool' and including the grinding stone where she used to sing with her sister (pp. 71–4). This same family is discouraged by Ocol from visiting her; he tells Lawino that they 'smell horribly' and have 'terrible diseases' (p. 150). What worries Lawino most of all in the later sections is Ocol's destruction of the ties that bind his own family. The greatest damage that Ocol's political feud is doing in Lawino's eyes is the way it is harming 'the well-being of our homestead' (p. 197). Ocol not only avoids the visits of his mother by going to town (p. 152) but, in a moment of Christian enthusiasm, threatened to destroy the tree growing on his father's grave and was only just constrained by his mother from cutting it down (p. 158). Although the poem falls too readily into two halves, the first half dominated by Clementine and concerned with extremely concrete issues of womanly rivalry and the second almost entirely losing sight of Clementine and ranging wide and abstract over other issues, the portrait of Lawino is consistent and this clarity of focus on a woman ruled by pride and love of family is an important reason for the initial impact and overall success of the poem.

As well as finding the cultural champion Lawino inconsistent with Lawino as Clementine's rival, Okumo pa'Lukobo also criticizes the characterization for its lack of verisimilitude:

> Neither Lawino nor Ocol are recognizable as real people; they are caricatures. Lawino, instead of constructively defending the old ways, rejects everything that is new outright: even soap and penicillin, the modern home and money which are today's necessities.
> (op. cit.)

This criticism is a misreading of the poem. Lawino rarely rejects anything 'outright' as Ocol does. She does not, unlike Ocol, seek to force conformity to the patterns of life she thinks are right. Her purpose is primarily defensive and she asserts her tolerance of others' behaviour on two or three occasions; for example:

> I do not understand
> The ways of foreigners
> But I do not despise their customs
> Why should you despise yours? (p. 29)

She mocks many aspects of the behaviour of Westernized Africans but on other occasions she simply admits to incomprehension of the new techniques they use. She mocks tinned and processed food, but admits to fear and incompetence when faced with primus, charcoal and electric stoves. She mocks Ocol's obsessive attitude to time but admits to an inability to read the clock. She treads very warily on the subject of Western medicine, concentrating all her criticism of Ocol on his intolerance of traditional medicine and the superstitious nature of his Christianity. She is willing to admit that Western medicine is powerful, yet tells us she:

... cannot measure
The heat of the body
With the white man's glass rod ... (p. 159)

Okot's satire is two-edged: Lawino's admissions of incompetence are gentle satire of her by Okot. Lawino does not reject 'outright' those machines and techniques she is afraid of, she merely begs to be allowed to continue to use the old ways she does understand.

Lawino does not have the grotesque outlines usually associated with caricature. The springs of her characterization are plausible and the range of her moods is human. Nevertheless, there is an important implausible aspect of the portrait which lies behind Okumu pa'Lukobo's insistence on her unreality. He expresses this criticism better earlier in the essay when he comments on Lawino's ignorance and dislike of the ballroom dance:

> These lines make Lawino into a complete outsider. For I know of no place in Acoli today where the village girls can't dance at least a sort of rumba: and Congolese records are the talk of young people in every household. (op. cit.)

This is valid criticism and could be applied with only a little less force to other things; Lawino should be able to 'tune the radio' (p. 47), she should be more familiar with vaccination, with soap, and with telling the time. She is ultra-conservative. This element of implausibility reduces the realism of the portrait but it does not affect the major issues of Lawino's motivation and the bases of her conflict with Ocol and Clementine.

Because in *Song of Lawino* we only know what Lawino chooses to tell us about Ocol, there is some difficulty in disentangling the characterization of Ocol from that of Lawino. How far is the reader intended to accept Lawino's reportage of what Ocol says and does as accurate, and how far can we assume that she exaggerates Ocol's behaviour because of her own obsessions? Writing of *Song of Lawino* before the publication of *Song of Ocol* in an essay, 'The Patriot as Artist', Ali Mazrui elaborates this question:

> If Lawino's account of her husband is correct, Okot has merely succeeded in creating a caricature that could in no way be regarded as representative of the type of person he wants to typify. Ocol by this account is a hyperbolic deserter from his own culture. The person lacks full credibility. On the other hand, if the exaggeration is supposed to be a method of characterizing Lawino's mind rather than of giving us the real picture of her husband, again p'Bitek only succeeds in making Lawino a little too simple. A mind that exaggerates so much and in such an obvious way is not simply *culturally* distinct from the modernity which enchants Ocol; it is also a mind too naïve to stand a chance of saving Ocol from that enchantment.

(Ali Mazrui, 'The Patriot as Artist', in G. D. Killam (ed.), *African Writers on African Writing*, p. 85)

Lawino is not as 'naïve' as Mazrui suggests she may be. Although there is likely to be some exaggeration, particularly in the early sections, it can be assumed that Ocol has done and said most of the things she describes. For the portrayal of Ocol, the poem can be divided into three parts, in each of which Ocol is dominated by a different ruling passion. In Sections 2 to 5, Ocol appears almost exclusively as the consort of Clementine, showering expensive gifts on her, attending her to dances, and expressing his loyalty to her by his ill-treatment of Lawino. In Sections, 6, 8, 9 and 10 he is the most devoted of mission boys with one eye always fixed nervously on his white master to make sure he doesn't deviate a millimetre from the prescribed way. In Sections 7 and 11 he is a self-important man of affairs, his nervous eye now trained upon the clock and his political masters who dominate his days as much as the white man's image does in other sections.

As with the different aspects of Lawino, there is no irreconcilable contradiction between these roles in themselves but minor contradictions arise from some of the 'hyperbolic' details of the portrait. Okumu pa'Lukobo justifies his description of Ocol as a 'caricature' (quoted above p. 71) by picking out some of these details:

> Ocol wears a blanket suit in the middle of the hot season, rejects Acoli names and threatens the ancestral shrine with an axe.
> (Okumu pa'Lukobo, op. cit.)

The condemnation of Acoli names and the threat to the shrine must be taken seriously and these attitudes contradict other aspects of Ocol's personality. Such an enthusiastic Christian would be repelled by the kind of overcrowded dancehall where couples kiss as they dance (p. 36) which, Lawino implies, is one of Ocol's regular haunts. Similarly, a Democratic Party politician must be a good Catholic and also a good nationalist (see below, p. 111), as Ocol is in his condemnation of 'White people' for 'the forced labour system' (p. 171). But his insistence on the eradication of 'pagan' names and projected desecration of holy places sits uneasily on an 'educated' African Christian of Mbiti's generation;[3] they belong to an earlier generation of convert. As Lawino is ultra-conservative in some of her peasant attitudes, Ocol is out of date in some of his Christian attitudes, but whereas in its motivation Lawino's character is plausible, for Ocol the extravagant gestures remain implausible because their roots in his past are much more weakly drawn and so the contradictions are not reconciled.

We learn of Ocol partly through Lawino's reportage of his words, partly through her descriptions of his behaviour now, and partly through his appearance in a very few anecdotes about the past. Once Section 1 has established a conventional mould for Ocol through the vocabulary he uses, key words like 'primitive', 'kaffirs' and 'sorcerers' describing those he attacks, and 'modern . . . progressive and civilized' describing himself, the attitudes expressed in the few lines which launch Lawino into most of Sections 2 to 10 are entirely predictable. Ocol is not given a sufficient say for a more rounded picture of him to emerge; only Lawino's descriptions of his present behaviour bring him to life a little more. Ocol spends a lot of his time 'sitting in his sofa', reading, an activity which Lawino despises because it is so silent, and when any noise disturbs him he is wildly angry. His obsession with punctuality arises from his sense of his own importance but it only mystifies Lawino because she thinks haste is undignified and because he can spare no time for telling tales around the evening fire or even for those who visit him (pp. 92–5). Section 9 confirms this picture of non-communicative home life. Ocol refuses to answer Lawino's questions about the creation because she is not 'educated' and avoids her eyes 'And talks casually / While doing some other work' (p. 142). Section 11 contains the same elements of futile attempts to break down a barrier of non-communication, this time with all the villagers at the political meeting (pp. 192–4), and of his busy-ness destroying rather than adding to his dignity because of his fawning before the leaders from Kampala (p. 191).

The personality of Ocol in these sections is that of a man, prominent in his local society, impelled by some deep-seated sense of insecurity to reassert his importance, who only succeeds in making himself look foolish. This personality is consistent with all Ocol's behaviour in the poem, but the portrait lacks any illustration of what has caused his insecurity. The roots of Lawino's present concerns are clear from her anecdotes of the past, but Ocol very rarely appears in these anecdotes and when he does they fail to add to our understanding of his character. Lawino's descriptions of their courtship and honeymoon periods in Sections 2 and 4 tell us nothing about Ocol except that he loved her devotedly and Section 4 is notable for her greater nostalgic interest in her old home than for any details of their courtship. Section 8 contains no parallel description of Ocol's youthful attitudes to the missionaries to contrast with Lawino's rejection of their meaningless phrases (p. 117), and the incident at his father's shrine illustrates an obsession that had already been fixed rather than showing how Ocol came to be obsessed. Ocol is more a 'caricature' than a plausible character, not so much because of his 'hyperbolic' desertion of his culture as because of the absence of clearly portrayed springs of motivation for his behaviour.

Of the three aspects of Ocol present in *Song of Lawino*, one, that of the busy man of affairs, the politician, dominates in *Song of Ocol*. The religious enthusiasm of *Song of Lawino* is in no way hinted at; Ocol puts his faith for the future in the brute technology which can destroy not only the traditional customs of East Africa, but also its landscape, in the cause of progress:

> We will uproot
> Each tree
> From the Ituri forest
> And blow up
> Mount Kilimanjaro, (p. 73)

Nowhere in the poem are spiritual trimmings added to this rapacious recipe. The 'superstitions' Ocol mentions irritate him because they are 'stagnant mud' in which Africans are 'stuck' on their road to progress (p. 20), not because of their conflict with Christianity. The tone of the whole poem is consistent with Ocol as a busy public figure: in Section 6 he is clearly a politician (p. 56) and a prominent member of the 'Party' addressing his constituents, while at the end of the poem he appears in the Parliament addressing the 'President', the 'Speaker', and his fellow MPs (p. 81).

He appears to have grown considerably in stature since the campaigning described in Section 11 of *Song of Lawino*, because the local party leader, especially of the declining opposition Democratic Party, who is so dependent on the good will of the big men in Kampala, could hardly have accumulated quite so much property as he displays in Section 6 of *Song of Ocol* (pp. 57–62). His claim to be among the 'brothers-in-power' (p. 55) is similarly inconsistent with the opposition role of the Democratic Party, but the contradiction can be resolved since many Democratic Party members crossed the floor of the house in the mid-sixties. Though the two-party system still seems to be in operation, as Ocol mentions the 'Opposition Chiefs' (p. 81), party politics appears to be very much a dead issue, unlike in *Song of Lawino*. The personality of Ocol in *Song of Ocol* alone is totally consistent. Taking his character in the two poems together, there seems to be a considerable jump forward in time, in that the out-of-date mission-boy attitudes are abandoned completely and replaced by the dedicated pursuit of the holy grail of 'progress'. Moreover, Ocol's fawning dependence on the favours of the greatest in the land has borne fruit, despite the initial setback of joining the wrong party.

Ocol the politician in *Song of Ocol* is too honest. Instead of discovering the roots of his character through the ambiguities of admission and denial we saw in relation to Lawino in Section 2 of *Song of Lawino* (see above, p. 67), Ocol exposes them to us in Section 2 of his 'Song', raw and bleeding, with a perception in self-analysis and a directness of self-revelation that is utterly implausible. Throughout the poem Ocol expresses not the likely public face of a political leader in black Africa, but what Okot considers to be the attitudes behind what the political leaders do. As with the springs of motivation of Ocol in *Song of Lawino*, we are told these attitudes rather than shown them in action. A black politician is not likely to confess to shame at his own blackness (p. 22) or trample on the intellectual symbols of reborn black pride as he does at the end of Section 3 (pp. 30–1). He would not publicly express contempt for the efforts of his supporters in the constituency and then disclaim responsibility for their poverty (pp. 56–7), nor, least of all, would he promise the world to name streets after white explorers as Ocol does in Section 9 (p. 85). Perhaps the nearest dramatic analogy to Ocol in *Song of Ocol* is of a Machiavellian villain in soliloquy standing outside the dramatic situation created by *Song of Lawino* to goad the various members of his East African audience from a standpoint of unregenerate villainy for their helpless or hypocritical sympathy for Lawino.

Though in Lawino Okot has created a plausible character, a number of aspects of *Song of Lawino* and *Song of Ocol* suggest that her plausibility was incidental rather than central to the poet's purpose. His strict adherence to a thematic structure means that many of the anecdotes which bring her to life appear late in the poem and are therefore not as effective in enlivening some parts of the conflict of ideas as they could be. The abrupt disappearance of Clementine and the apparent shift of emphasis from pride in womanly accomplishments to concern for family life and its values lay the poet open to charges of inconsistency in characterization which could easily have been avoided. Okot makes no attempt to emulate the fullness of his portrayal of Lawino in his characterization of either Ocol or Clementine. In both poems, Ocol's behaviour is inconsistent in minor ways which the poet could easily have reconciled by providing a little more information about his background. Although a lot of Okot's popularity as a poet can be attributed to the vividness of Lawino as a plausible individual, he is not concerned that his characters should be seen as individuals. He is much more interested in them as satiric representatives of social types. I discuss the poems as satire in Chapters 6, 7 and 8.

In the Introduction to the American edition of *Song of a Prisoner*, Edward Blishen says that the poem contains several masks for the poet and asserts that:

> The prisoner cannot be read as a single character. At times he is a kind of Patrice Lumumba, being beaten to the point of death; a betrayed hero of Uhuru. At other times he seems to be any political detainee, imprisoned for his opinions or political actions. Again, he is an assassin, who has rid his country of a tyrant; who pretends wildly not to understand why his captors do not form a guard of honour for him.
> (*Song of a Prisoner*, Introduction, p. 31)

In her essay on 'Song of Prisoner' Margaret Marshment rejects Edward Blishen's interpretation in favour of her own view of the prisoner as an ironically characterized individual:

> The Prisoner *is* a single character: he has a specific biography which we are told in the poem: he has a home, a wife who has been seduced by a rich man with a Mercedes, children who are suffering from hunger and disease; he fought for Uhuru, he was a bodyguard; and now he is still poor and has assassinated a political leader.
> (*Standpoints on African Literature*, p. 128)

There is enough of a fictional outline to make the whole 'Song' one poem and not, as Edward Blishen calls it, a 'sequence' (*Song of a Prisoner*, Introduction, p. 33) but there is more than one voice in the poem and the main prisoner's biography is not as clear cut as Margaret Marshment believes. Blishen does not explain the masks he mentions in any other way than in the paragraph above. The contradictions he raises there can easily be resolved. Blishen fails to make any allowance for the possibility of confusion or even mild self-deception on the prisoner's part. He takes the prisoner's view of himself as 'a betrayed hero of Uhuru' as a fact associated with one of the masks in the poem and, on the basis of the poem's dedication and not on internal evidence, links this mask with Patrice Lumumba.[4] The only political action mentioned in the poem is the assassination and the only political opinions expressed are a justification of that assassination, yet Blishen separates the assassination from other unspecified 'opinions or . . . political actions' which belong to another mask in the poem. Who is and is not a hero of Uhuru in contemporary Africa is decidedly a matter of opinion and an assassin, even a hired assassin ('I did not do it / For the money', p. 67), is likely to see himself as one even if no one else shares his view. Blishen has not established the existence of three separate masks.

There are two inconsistencies that Blishen does not raise, both concerned with Sections 8 to 12, which are more difficult to resolve. In his review of *Two Songs*, Richard Ntiru raises one of them when he describes the poem as:

> . . . a prisoner's self-defence in which the evidence is sometimes confused and sometimes blatantly contradictory. . . . His guilt shifts from vagrancy when he is talking to his warder . . . to assassination of a corrupt leader who is purportedly leading the country astray.
> (R. C. Ntiru, review of *Two Songs*, in *East Africa Journal*, pp. 39–40)

At the beginning of the poem, the prisoner confesses to vagrancy, but refuses to acknowledge that it is a crime:

Why should I not
Sleep with the green grass
In the City Park
While I nurse
My hunger?
Why do they call me
A vagrant
A loiterer? (pp. 15–16)

The first six sections do not link the prisoner with political action of any sort but underline his poverty by the pictures of his starving children and the condemnation of his mother and father. It thus seems possible that vagrancy is the only crime in question and that he is suffering from his warders' sadism rather than from planned torture, except for the one false note of the courtroom question:

Do you plead
Guilty
Or
Not guilty? (p. 12)

It suggests that he has been accused of a more serious crime to which he has not confessed and this is confirmed later when he decides that he 'will plead / Not guilty' and so 'will not be hanged'. Hanging is too severe a punishment for vagrancy and a defence against vagrancy could not under any circumstances involve 'The best lawyer' (p. 59).

Sections 8, 9 and 10 are radically different in tone, being 'The triumphant song' of someone who sees himself as 'the hero of Uhuru' (p. 66) who begins with a confession that he killed a leader:

Yes
I did it
And,
My God,
What a beautiful
Shot! (p. 66)

The assassin admits that he was hired but still attempts to justify the crime, first apparently to the warders who are beating him and then to the widow of the murdered man. After that he loses himself in a vision of public acclaim for his 'great deed' (p. 79). In Section 11 the voice we hear most of the time is of someone who calls himself 'a Minister' (p. 82) and bewails his fall from a position of great wealth, and the diplomatic party in Section 12 is in the same kind of environment. Section 13 emphatically returns to the earlier village world and although in Sections 14 and 15 the prisoner's general knowledge and imaginative projections are first world-wide and then pan-African, these sections are also tied to a poor man with the reference to the 'children' who 'will never go to school' (p. 109) and to the role of 'bodyguard' (p. 117) near the very end of the poem. From this analysis there seem to be three possible reasons for the imprisonment of the person (or people) whose voice (or voices) we hear: vagrancy, political assassination, and a political squabble within a cabinet or a coup which led to the disgrace and imprisonment of a minister.

The one dissatisfaction Bahadur Tejani expresses with the poem in his review concerns the role of the 'Minister' in the poem:

> In the last five sections of the poem, Okot tries a complex experiment, of contrasting the inner life of a 'Minister' with that of the prisoner. Somehow this doesn't quite come off, simply because it is difficult to judge who is who. (Bahadur Tehani, review of *Two Songs*, in Eldred Jones (ed.), *African Literature Today, No. 6, Poetry in Africa*, p. 162)

Margaret Marshment also hints at mild dissatisfaction with the lack of clarity surrounding the minister but gives him a dramatic role as a noise from outside the cell coming in to the prisoner and a possible role in the prisoner's biography as his employer:

> Here Section 11, 'Soft Grass' is relevant. Okot tells me that this is the voice of a man in the next cell, whom the prisoner overhears. This was not clear to me, and we could wish it were clearer because it is important. . . . But we can guess at one reason why he might be in prison: that he was the assassin's employer.
> (*Standpoints on African Literature*, pp. 134–5)

The separateness of the minister's voice is not indicated sufficiently clearly; Okot's verbal footnote to Margaret Marshment was necessary, although there is some evidence to support the idea of two voices. Section 11 opens with the vagrant studying a millipede and 'her newly hatched baby' and this quiet occupation is interrupted by the minister's screams. The vagrant's first reaction is to tell the minister not to make noises that 'disturb / The sleeping one' (p. 81). The minister's voice takes over for most of the rest of the section, but the vagrant appears to interpolate his own comments on the minister's predicament several times. Although animal images are common throughout the poem, they are nowhere else so frequent as they are in this section. The picture of interrupted contemplation and the interweaving of shouts of pain with dry commentary are consistent with Margaret Marshment's view.

The minister clearly has a different biography from the vagrant as his father is apparently alive, his children are at school, and both his parents are accustomed to receiving cheques from him (p. 87).

Tejani's description of the minister is different from Marshment's. He spreads the supposed references to the minister vaguely over 'the last five sections' and talks of the minister's 'inner life' rather than his overheard ravings. Section 12 supports Tejani's view of the more diffuse presence of the minister because it is closer to his imagination than to that of the vagrant. The voice speaks confidently to the 'pressmen of the world' (p. 90), expects servility from waiters (p. 92), is very concerned with freedom of speech (p. 90), and talks of 'the old woman / In my constituency' (p. 92). This is also one of the very few sections with no reference to a poverty-stricken family. This voice must be that of the minister and the absence of any hint of another interpretative voice suggests that we are now in the minister's 'inner life' rather than overhearing his shouted protests. There is no cause to see the minister's presence anywhere in the remainder of the poem.

Looking at the contrast between the vagrant and the self-assured assassin in the earlier part of the poem suggests the existence of yet another prisoner, again overheard by the original vagrant. The title of Section 8, 'distant echoes', may itself imply an overheard voice and its structure is similar to Section 11. It begins with the vagrant's contemplation of the '*lek* lizard', linked through the image of 'The sharks of Uhuru' to the violence in society around him (pp. 65–6). Then, more explicitly than in Section 11, he hears something from outside his cell:

> I hear
> The triumphant song
> Of the hero of Uhuru
> Listen to him (p. 66)

The alternation of loud protest with dry comment continues. Sections 9 and 10 are similar to Section 12 in that they express the 'inner world' of the assassin, the third prisoner, rather than that of the vagrant prisoner. If this interpretation is correct then the vagrant prisoner has been accused of the murder, he has been picked up on suspicion because he was sleeping in City Park and possibly because of his association with someone powerful for whom he has been bodyguard, but he is innocent. The crucial question relating to this interpretation is the ambiguous reference in Section 7, a section with no possible hint of two voices, to 'those who hired me' (p. 59). This sounds like a reference by an assassin to those who paid him for the killing, but it is possible that it is the vagrant prisoner talking of the man who employed him as a bodyguard. This ambiguity is a weakness in the fiction of the poem.

Even the vagrant's biography is not as clear as Margaret Marshment suggests (see above, p. 77) because his state of mind makes him an unreliable witness. The vagrant, like Richard II at Pomfret, has to 'people this little world' of his bare cell and, like Richard, he peoples it with 'still-breeding thoughts'. The music of the player outside the cell floats in and mingles with the king's lonely thoughts (*Richard II*, V, 5) and similarly the vagrant reacts to a number of noises from outside his cell and builds his fantasies around them. But Richard is not being tortured, his mind is clear and his personification of his thoughts is nothing more than an elaborate conceit. The vagrant, on the other hand, probably because of the torture he is suffering, cannot distinguish between fantasy and reality, and thus we cannot tell which things are true within the internal fiction of the poem and which are only the vagrant's fantasies. Section 3 illustrates the way fantasy, the present reality, and memories are confused and intermingled. The refreshing noise of the rain outside the vagrant's cell is interrupted by the 'haughty horns' of the guards' 'jeers' before they come in to attack him. His pain is first expressed through the trumpeting and screaming of elephants and rhinos. Then it is transferred to what may be a memory, but is probably a fantasy, of an invasion of his village by tanks, machine guns, and bombers against the spears and buffalo-hide shields of the defenders until he is left in his helplessness in his own mess on the wet floor (pp. 29–34). Section 5 begins with a description of the prisoner coming to himself in the 'black silence' of his cell, moving from the physical discomfort of his position and the pain in his head to the worst of his injuries, his bleeding penis which has attracted the warders' most sadistic attention. It is the idea of his own impotence that provokes the vivid mental picture of the rape of his wife by the 'Big Chief' with the 'Benz' and the violent desire to drink 'Human blood' to cool his rage (pp. 34–47). Sections 4 and 6 and the last three sections are largely fantasies.

The vagrant uses the past tense about himself on only three occasions: two references tell us of his physical skills, as a footballer, and boxer and hunter (pp. 13–14), and later as a dancer (p. 102), and one tells us of his most recent use of these skills as 'bodyguard' and organizer of political meetings (p. 117). Although he talks of his father and mother in the past tense, all his other descriptions of events involving himself are in the present tense and therefore easily open to interpretation as fantasies since the prisoner is confined to his cell throughout the poem. From these isolated facts, it seems that the prisoner started life and came to adulthood in a village and later moved to the town where the only role we know him to have had is that of toughie in a politician's entourage, warding off blows aimed at the leader (p. 117). His wife and children are still in the village in all his fantasies about them: they sleep in an old hut with leaking thatch (p. 60), without schooling his children will grow up 'With the wild trees / Of the bush' (p. 101), and his wife cooks over a fire

(p. 22). The vagrant's experiences in the town have made virtually no impression on his imagination: his family and village are mentioned in every section except the last one. At first he imagines them to be involved in his suffering, either remembering their troubles to mix with his own or transferring his pain to them. Later, when his fantasies become escapist and reach into the future, his family and clansmen appear in them. The farm he has bought is for his wife and children (p. 60) and before he seeks to dance and forget (pp. 105–8) he wants to dance and remember his wife, his clansmen, and his father whose shrine must be made a feasting place for 'the assembled ghosts / Of the dead' (p. 103). This biographical outline is very slight but it cannot justifiably be extended further. Margaret Marshment, in her summary biography of the prisoner, takes the seduction of the vagrant's wife by the Big Chief as a fact from the vagrant's past, but if it has just happened it is difficult to see how he can know about it and if it happened before his imprisonment it should be described in the past tense. Its juxtaposition next to the vagrant's discovery of his injured penis gives the description a clear *raison d'être* if it is considered as a fantasy.

The vagrant holds the poem together; the other two prisoners are seen through their effect on him. At the beginning of the poem he is fighting against despair despite the sadistic treatment whose cause he does not fully understand. He achieves a degree of self-delusory calmness when he visualizes 'The farm / In the fertile valley' (p. 60); then he hears the voices of two people who, as the true murderer and as a minister in the Uhuru government, are indirectly responsible for his predicament. In the last three sections, no longer tortured but still held in prison and apparently bound hand and foot (p. 102), he demands his release, firstly to express his 'pride' (p. 100) in his role within his own clan and then to forget his despair of his role within the new city. This is an essentially dramatic structure in that there is dramatic action through the torture and the voice or voices from outside the cell which affect the emotions and modify the attitudes of the main singer in the course of the poem.

In spite of the importance of this fictional structure, Okot is very careless about the internal fiction of the poem. Much more descriptive detail goes into what are almost certainly fantasies than into information about the past of the prisoners and there are inconsistencies in the information we are given. In Section 7 the vagrant tells his wife to 'Dream about our first meeting / In the forest' (p. 58), yet in Section 13 the same man talks of 'our first meeting / At the dancing arena' (p. 102). These first meetings are not even as specifically visualized as the one moment of nostalgia in *Song of Ocol*, where Ocol recalls the '*byeyo* tree' under which he first met Lawino with the sounds of the forest all around them (p. 77). Like most biographical details of the vagrant or assassin they are merely formulae that suggest the nostalgia of an alienated man for his rural home. 'Song of Prisoner' confirms the impression given by the other poems that Okot is more interested in the portrayal of social types than of individuals.

Notes to Chapter 5

1. The word 'malaya' is Swahili for 'prostitute' and is sometimes used in East African English.
2. Clementine only appears by name in Section 5, but the other three sections imply comparisons with her if we assume that she can 'dance the ballroom dance' (p. 35), 'hear Swahili or Luganda' (p. 47), and use 'White men's cooking stoves' (p. 66).
3. John Mbiti, though a Christian theologian, is a student of African religious concepts in which he finds many parallels to Christian beliefs. See *African Religions and Philosophy*, London: Heinemann Educational Books, 1969.
4. The East African edition is dedicated to Patrice Lumumba; the American edition to 'lumumba mondale kimathi mboya tshombe balewa . . . and for the bruised others'.

6 Satirical Techniques

IN view of Okot's dependence on the traditions of oral literature in relation to the form and verbal content of his 'Songs', a comparison between his method of dealing with the fictional aspect of his poetry and the methods used by oral performers seems worthwhile. The close relationship between composer/performer and audience in oral literature creates a more constant awareness of what Frye calls the 'external fiction' of 'a relation between the writer and the writer's society' (see above, p. 60) than is present in oral literature. In none of the literary forms of the Acoli is there a parallel to the tendency towards realism which has been so influential in European literature,[1] the attempt to submerge awareness of the relationship between writer and reader (the 'external fiction') in an 'internal fiction' which mimics real life in all its details. Some literary forms have very slight fictional elements and the most developed fictional forms, myths and tales told around the fire in the homestead, contain highly implausible elements, either in the magical powers of legendary heroes or the exaggerated fantasies that are a part of satire. There is a very strong tendency towards satire which sometimes spreads beyond the tales and *orak* dance songs where satire is the norm and affects other forms. Okot's satirical methods have been very much influenced by the methods of Acoli satirists.

In relation to the different types of oral literature discussed in Chapter 1 (see above, pp. 5–11), the 'external fiction' is strongest in the 'chants at the ancestral shrine' where the distinction between external and internal fiction is meaningless. The Chants dramatize the situation of the whole community of the clan who are involved in the ritual both as singers and as subjects of the prayers for good health, childbirth, hunting success, and other things. Similarly, the songs of the spirit possession dance dramatize the activities of the *jok* whose presence is causing the illness, of the diviner who cures him, and the conflict between them, which results in a real physical cure for real people. In the funeral songs there is a clearer distinction in that the participants in the *guru lyel* ceremony, many months after the death of the person being remembered, dramatize various stages of grief and a variety of different attitudes which the relatives of the dead man have already gone through. For the mock attack which every group makes on its arrival at the homestead of the dead person, that homestead becomes 'the homestead of Death's mother' (see above, p. 9) and the attackers take on the heroic dramatic status of warriors fighting against personified Death, their biggest enemy.

The funeral songs Okot calls 'Songs of the pathway' dramatize the moment of the discovery of the death of a loved one, when 'the mourner refuses to believe that the one he or she loved so much is no more' (*Horn of My Love*, p. 144). For a woman awaiting her lover it is the moment when she hears the distinctive notes of other men's horns as they return from battle and goes a little way along the path to greet her man, but never hears his horn:

Awinyo bila pa meya,
Oto Cura koni bineo,
Bila pare okok odiko con.
Omera, angiyo kwe
Ki i wanga yo do!
Ah, Cura koni oo,
Bila pare okok odiko con.

I heard the horn of my love,
Oto Cura will soon come,
His horn sounded early in the morning.
But I search for my brother in vain
Along the pathway, oh!
Ah, Cura will soon be here,
His horn sounded early in the morning.
(*Horn of My Love*, p. 119)

As with the chants at the ancestral shrine, the whole community participates in at least part of the dramatized action and the emotions dramatized are real and recent experiences of people within the community, but the fictional aspect is stronger in that there is a deliberate projection backwards in time into a succession of emotions by those who take part in the funeral.

Otole dances, similarly, are dramatic acts miming acts of war in which the whole of the chiefdom participates, both through the storming of the village by the visiting chiefdom, and through the struggles for dominance of one group's rhythm and the mock fights within the dancing arena. A new kind of 'internal fiction' is introduced as the songs elaborate on a known historical event and the singers sometimes assume the character of a figure involved in that event through the words of the song. Though each song dramatizes or recounts only a part of a significant event and does not provide a full narrative, Okot suggests that they are important historical documents because, when the elders meet to discuss a chiefdom's history:

> The song plays a vital role in their discussions, because it is the core of the discussion. Indeed, the history of a chiefdom is usually reconstructed through the songs.
> (*Horn of My Love*, p. 156)

Okot gives four such reconstructed histories in *Horn of My Love* (see pp. 156–67). The Palaro chiefdom consisted of a number of 'small but warlike clans' (ibid., p. 161) and had a complex history of disputes with many larger groups and a consequent pride in their capacity to strike fear into a large army with only a small group of warriors; this song concerns a particular battle with some Lang'o invaders:

Palaro gin acel, aryo . . .
Otingo polo ki tere;
Ee, Lango ringo,
Otingo polo ki tere;
Palaro gin acel aryo . . .

The host of Palaro, only a few, you can count them . . .
Lifted the sky from its base;
Ee, the Lango fled;
They lifted the sky from its base.
The host of Palaro, only a few, you can count them . . .
(ibid., p. 101)

The chief function of the songs is to celebrate the history of the chiefdom. The songs recall to the participants a known historical sequence of events which is in some ways the subject of the *otole* dance but which is not formally retold or re-enacted by the singers and dancers, but may be discussed by the elders from both chiefdoms, observing the dance.

The songs deal with a historical rather than a legendary world in that heroes display none of the magical attributes that are present in the myths. Although it is difficult to judge the verbal element of the songs alone, because they are incomplete without a knowledge of the historical background from which they arise and without the dance and the battle mime which is part of the literary event, the range of characterization is considerably greater than in the apparently fixed stock of responses to death of the funeral songs. Chiefs may be pictured as wise or foolish, brave or cowardly, strong or subservient to others who are stronger. The unmarried warriors or wives or mothers whose voices are assumed in some of the songs may support their chiefs or attempt to dissuade them and may shiver with fear or thrill with pride at the prospect of battle. A major aim of the songs is to express the characteristics of the chiefdom and this leads to hyperbole in describing the courage of one's own warrior or the cowardice of the enemy; but another important feature is the preservation of the memory of the real events of the chiefdom's history and so failure can be remembered, as in the Bwobo song which confesses:

Lweny ki Lango tek;
Lweny ki Lango oloya ye;
Kany ma adok kwene?

Fighting the Lango is difficult;
I have failed to fight the Lango, oh,
Where shall I go now?
(ibid., p. 157)

Myths recount the origins and justify the social divisions and some of the customs of a group of chiefdoms, a chiefdom, or a clan, through the deeds of chiefs and chiefs' sons, or, for commoner clans, of long-dead legendary ancestors. All these men are imbued with magical powers. Thus the birth of Labongo the great grandson of Lwo, the first man, is recounted as a miracle in the myth of Labongo. His mother went looking for firewood and never returned and could not be found until:

Nino mo Kilak otuc paco
Kome onongo pek
Kilak onywalo latin laco, Labongo
Latin onongo tangu
Kinyalo ki gara i tyene ki kono i wiye
Ticce myel

One day Kilak broke into homestead
Her body was heavy
(she was pregnant)
Kilak gave birth to a male child, Labongo
That child was a miracle
He was born with bells on his legs
and feathers on his head
His preoccupation was dancing
('Oral Literature Among the Acoli and Lang'o', p. 44)

Similarly the dispute over the succession to the stool of Labongo was settled by the successful performance of the three magic tasks of making a cow bear a calf with a forked tail, sucking beer through a solid stick, and striking two hoes together so that they stuck and could not be pulled apart (ibid., pp. 49–52). The myth of Okot's own clan, the Pa-Cua commoner clan, recounts how a *beyo* tree bent down its branches and lifted a man up in them and *okongo* birds sang a war alarm to frighten away the enemies that besieged this distant ancestor, thereby saving him from certain death (ibid., pp. 61–4). Myths contain complete 'internal fictions' but they are implausible because of the magical powers of the characters in them.

The tales told around the fire in the homestead are also complete narratives. They relate very closely to their audience in the style of their telling (see above, p. 6). They are radically different in the attitude of performer and audience from the myths. The force that breathes life into the ogre Obibi or the dwarf Lagitin, or causes Hare and his friends to act as human beings is not the magic that lends myths their solemn authority but the fantasy that is a component of satire. Okot tells us that the animals represent different types of human behaviour and the tales are 'a means of conveying moral messages' ('Oral Literature Among the Acoli and Lang'o', p. 419). They thus contain the elements of 'at least a token fantasy' and 'at least an implicit moral standard' (Northrop Frye, *Anatomy of Criticism*, p. 224) which are the hallmarks of satire. In representing the human situation through the actions of animals the story teller offers his hearers, in the words of Matthew Hodgart, not 'pure realism' but 'a travesty of the situation' (Matthew Hodgart, *Satire*, p.12). The skill of the teller therefore presumably lies in striking the correct balance between the grotesque exaggeration inherent in the use of the animal type and that degree of real imitation of the satirized individual necessary to make the satire bite on its victim. Full explanation of all the meanings of a satire always demands a commentary on the people satirized and their historical situation which, in relation to these folk tales, would require participation in the life of the community concerned for months or years before the tale was told. Nevertheless too rigid a functional approach may well tend to exaggerate the morality inherent in the tales and therefore under-emphasize both the entertainment value and the realism possible in the hands of a good story teller.[2] Okot's account of how the affair of Hare sleeping with his mother-in-law would be handled in front of an adult audience indicates strong tendencies to suppress the fantasy and express the tale in more realistic terms:

> ... you hear a detailed description of the background of Hare's mother-in-law: her age, what she was like in her youth—a loose girl? Were her parents or brothers too strict? etc. You are also told exactly how it is that Hare came to commit such a crime, the various stages from when he first made his advance to the actual sexual act; the various methods and styles of

making love secretly are described and their advantages and disadvantages discussed openly, frankly, etc.
('Oral Literature Among the Acoli and Lang'o', p, 393)

The implication is not only that there is a sexual realism which necessitates totally losing sight of Hare's animal identity but that there is an element of psychological realism tracing the origins of this crime back into the past and implying causes elsewhere in the life of the community. The predominant mode of characterization is still that of caricature as is appropriate to satire.

In addition to the 'travesty' as a form of satire, Matthew Hodgart also identifies the 'lampoon or personal attack' (*Satire*, p. 14) as another basic form. Whilst Acoli lampoons are considerably more sophisticated in their wit than Hodgart's analysis of 'primitive' lampoons (ibid., pp. 14–20) would suggest the lampoon is very important as a type of Acoli song. No occasion appears to be too solemn for the use of personal attacks on people; the competition over the inheritance which comes at the end of the *guru lyel* ceremony may involve fairly bitter mocking attack, as in the song '*Ceng ma too peke*' (see above, p. 17). Similarly when the chiefs lost their traditional status and became agents of the British administration, even a *bwola* song could be used to mock a chief:

Yee kop ma owaco ma nok
Rwot Olal ming
Tero nyinga bot Munu ne
Ka doto an
Yee—laroro
Tero nyinga bot Orunga
Ka cato ne

Oh! the little words [unimportant] I say
Chief Olal is so foolish
He takes [reports] my name to his white boss
To accuse me
Oh! dangerous gossiper
Takes my name to Oringa [nickname for the DC]
To sell it [the information]
('Oral Literature Among the Acoli and Lang'o', p. 121)

The songs at the *orak* dance are almost entirely lampoons. They may attack a wide variety of personal faults from the most trivial to the most serious. The next song attacks a girl for her inability to wriggle her waist while turning around in front of the boys at the dance, that is, to do the *teke*:

Nyama wiro dude awira
Lanyami teke dong' peke
Nya pa Maro
Loko dude aloka ye
Lamin apwai
Teke oloyo anyaka do!

This girl simply turns her buttocks
This girl, to do the *teke* she cannot
Daughter of a mother-in-law
She simply moves her buttocks
Sister of the youth
Teke she is completely unable to do oh!
(ibid., p. 301)

The next song, at the other extreme, taunts a man because of his strange appearance with the accusation of witchcraft:

Wuyeny yat mutwo
Wurwak i ter Owiny
Twora Lunyama do!
Twora Lunyama ya
Neno yat mutal
Guru ter Owiny
Otyeko jo ki tal tal
Twon lajok ya

Look for a dry peg
Push it into Owiny's anus
Lunyama is far less dangerous oh!
Lunyama is far less dangerous
Get a stout dry peg
Drive it into Owiny's anus
He has finished many people with his sorcery
He is a great wizard.
(ibid., p. 309)

Although these songs are much more local in the community they reach than *otole* or *bwola* songs, they reach a much wider audience than do the folk tales. Whatever the level of behaviour they criticize, the use of lampoon rather than animal fantasy gives the songs a sharper cutting edge, especially in the highly competitive courtship arena of the *orak* dance. Mention in an *orak* song is feared:

> Very few of them sing praises; the so-called love songs are often a combination of praise and insult. . . . The fear of being a subject of these songs acts as an important sanction. The dancers and watchers come from a small locality. They usually know who the subject of the dance is; and an *orak* song from one area is soon known in another area of the locality. A person becomes well known, but not for the good things he has done. To be a subject of an *orak* song is not a thing to be proud of, no one desires it.
> (ibid., pp. 314–15)

The verbal content of these songs is more independent of other forms of dramatization in that there is no mime parallel to the acts of war which are an essential feature of *otole* songs. It is in relation to these songs that the *lucak wer*, the composer/performers, come into their own, being 'well known, feared and respected' with considerable status and influence in the community because of their acknowledged ability to lampoon their enemies (ibid., p. 291). The lampoon makes no attempt to tell the whole truth about a character. Even more than longer satirical forms it is selective, isolating a single characteristic of the victim for mockery and disregarding the distortion inherent in such selection. The singer of a lampoon deals with a situation largely familiar to his audience, he is always aware of that audience, and is frankly partisan in front of them, knowing that they may turn on him if he goes too far.

Whilst the 'internal fictions' in Okot's 'Songs' are fuller than those in any of the sung and therefore, by Okot's definition (see above, p. 6), the 'verse' forms in Acoli oral literature, and the only substantially fictional forms, the myths and folk tales, are narratives, Okot's disregard for the contemporary Western ideal of plausibility in fiction suggests the possibility of influences from oral literature on this area of his practice as a writer as well as on others. Lawino, Ocol, and the malaya can all be said to lampoon their enemies in something of the manner of the *lucak wer*. *Song of Lawino* is nearest to lampoon because much of its satire is concentrated on a single character, but it displays the tendency, also found in the other poems, to move from personal lampoon to satire on social groups. The ballroom dance is described using a vague impersonal plural ('You' or 'They') and a similar plural is used for parts of her condemnation of Ocol's ignorance of Acoli games and her mockery of Clementine's hair-straightening (*Song of Lawino*, pp. 35–40, 47–9, and 59–60). The only personal lampoon in *Song of Ocol* is his invective against Lawino's 'Song' in Section 1, and the malaya lampoons the Big Chief, the bishop, the teacher and her brother but the remainder of these songs generalize their satire to the social groups whom they address. In both personal lampoon and generalized satire many of the techniques of the *lucak wer* are used.

Most oral lampoons belong to what Northrop Frye calls the 'first phase' of satire which operates within a set of conventional social norms and 'does not question the logic of social convention' but recommends 'conventional life at its best. (Northrop Frye, *Anatomy of Criticism*, p. 226). They assume the existence of known standards of behaviour to which they can appeal and which they hope to restore by their satire. These songs often involve nothing more than the broadcasting of unwelcome facts about the victim with no distortion of the victim's behaviour or elaboration of the singer's attitude, as is the case in the song used to mock the girl who cannot 'do the *teke*' (see above p. 40) and in this criticism of a girl called Ato:

Oringo welo yo
Oringo welo dok Lumule
Oringo welo
Wi yo! Ato oringo welo
Ato woko
Ato oringo welo

She ran away from visitors
She ran away towards Nimule
She ran away from visitors
Oo dear! Ato ran away from visitors
I die (of shame)
Ato ran away from visitors
('Oral Literature Among the Acoli and Lang'o', p. 305)

Ato, Okot tells us, continued to go on a pre-arranged journey even though visitors arrived at the homestead shortly before her departure (loc. cit.). The only mild distortion in the satirist's account of this incident is the suggestion that Ato 'ran away'; no further elaboration of the discourtesy of her attitude is necessary. As long as the Acoli satirical song deals with the behaviour of individuals who fail to live up to the conventional norms expected of them, no more complex attitude to social convention or deviant behaviour is likely to be reflected in them, but when the behaviour satirized can be seen as typical of a new social attitude or a new social group the songs move into an area of conflict between differing sets of values and competing norms of behaviour.

The next song deals with the conflict between the desire for mobility and the love of machines that has grown in the last few decades with the old conventions which value marriage and children above all else:

Rii rii ye,
Rii rii ye,
Awinyo lela okok,

Lela okok kili,
Meno nya pa anga?
Lim kor Laker,
Lim kor lamera
Iwilo ki gari ba . . .

I hear a bicycle bell,
I hear a bicycle bell,
The bell sounded
It went kling, kling,
Whose daughter is that?
The bridewealth of Laker,
The bridewealth of my sister,
You use it for buying a bicycle . . .
(*Horn of My Love*, p. 78)[3]

The windfall of a sister's bridewealth is normally a major source of the money a brother needs to get married himself. The *lucak wer* asks '*Kelo dako bongo*?' 'Why does it [the bridewealth] not bring a woman home?'. Now the young man has used this money he will never be able to afford to marry and will be left with the bicycle as his wife. The singer ignores the benefits of the bicycle and the admiration it is likely to have excited amongst many of the young man's friends. He deals with a situation in which people are confused by two competing norms of behaviour simply by ignoring the existence of one of the norms. The bicycle is found to be useless because it cannot fulfil the role of a wife:

Wang lela peke,
Konyo dano bongo;

A bicycle has no eyes,
It cannot help your clansmen;
(loc. cit.)

Lawino and Ocol use a similar technique in their satire. Acoli society is caught between its old conventions and a number of imported norms which have won some acceptance over a period of a couple of generations. Most members of it are familiar with both sets of norms and therefore understand the behaviour of those whose life style has changed less or more than their own, even when they do not approve of it. Lawino and Ocol refuse to understand the behaviour they are mocking and remove it as far as possible from the situation in which it is meaningful to make fun of it.

Lawino's most subtle insinuations against Clementine's physical appearance are made by references to witchcraft and sorcery. Her painfully acquired slimness is compared to the appearance of someone who is suffering from a succession of diseases because of the activities of a shadow trapper (*Song of Lawino*, p. 26). The victims of these sorcerers 'wasted away . . . lost appetite and strength [and] . . . became dull and stupid' (*Religion of the Central Lao*, p. 133). Her long hair which makes her head look huge and the lipstick she uses give her the kind of eccentric appearance which might have led to accusations of witchcraft. Lawino pretends that she can only understand Clementine's fashionable appearance by reference to witchcraft and sorcery, an area of life very far removed from the modern houses and dancehalls where Clementine's behaviour appears normal. Her suggestion that Ocol is hiding skin diseases and his politician's paunch 'Like that of a pregnant goat' (p. 49) under his European suit is deliberate misunderstanding of the same type. Her treatment of the creation myth reflects a similar refusal to accept the existence of ideas which are now commonplace in her society. The mistranslations of the Acoli words for Father, Son and Holy Spirit (see above, p. 57) wrench the concepts out of their frame of reference and place them within the Acoli spirit world. The world 'mould' in place of 'create' arises from the same account of the confrontation between missionaries and elders and provides the idea of rewriting the myth as the story of a potter which occupies most of the section (pp. 138–45).

The whole of Ocol's treatment of women in *Song of Ocol* similarly distorts the position of African women by the selections and omissions in his description. Lawino's description of an Acoli woman's walk to the well with the 'long-necked jar' on her head (pp. 56–7) is degraded by Ocol's description of the same woman returning from the well with 'a large pot' on her head, the water spilling over her face (p. 35). The women are pictured only whilst working and the bridewealth is reduced to nothing but barter through the use of the words 'buy' and 'trade' in connection with it. In a similar way Ocol refuses to acknowledge the symbolic value of the paraphernalia of rural life. No cultural significance can save objects from his refining bonfire; they are always judged only by their technological inferiority to their Western equivalents. The horn with its individual notes (see above, p. 49) is compared to 'a sneezing hippo' (p. 34); people are to be punished for blowing them (p. 50). In the references to pastoral groups, spears appear mainly as weapons but also as symbols of manly identity, as when he talks of the Kalenjin who 'Sang songs about the might / Of your spears' (p. 48). As weapons, he tells us they 'Will be destroyed' (p. 50) and he mocks their symbolic value, calling the spear 'The symbol of your backwardness' (p. 48). Even the chief's spear is treated as nothing more than a weapon. He makes two brief references to the myth of Labongo and Gipir, first when he talks of Africa:

... following the spoor
Of the elephant
That he has speared
But could not kill; (p. 21)

Again at the end of the poem he condemns Labongo and Gipir for their 'quarrels / Over a spear' (p. 86).

The reduction of the stature and dignity of a satirist's victim is a major technique of satire and one form it often makes is the comparison of the victim to animals, birds, insects, and even to the vegetable and mineral. This song degrades a greedy chief by comparing him to 'termites':

Abucolom, cam bye bye neko dano
Abucolom camo labolo mupongo aduku lawang acel
Cam naka naka balo dano.

Abucolom, endless feeding like termites kills a man
Abucolom eats a whole basketful of bananas at one go
Eating endlessly spoils [the shape of] a man
('Oral Literature Among the Acoli and Lang'o', pp. 313–14)

Song of Lawino begins with a plethora of degrading non-human comparisons for people, including Ocol's abuse of Lawino and Lawino's attacks on both Clementine and Ocol. This level of invective is fortunately not sustained throughout the poem but there are some other examples (see pp. 117–18 and 59–60) and Ocol occasionally uses the same technique (see pp. 39–41, 60–1, 65, and 71). In relation to hair styles Lawino uses animal comparisons to contrast the images of different cultures of what is beautiful. On the surface, Lawino's point is that different racial groups have different textures of hair and therefore cannot imitate each others' hair styles and her first series of analogies illustrates nothing more than that:

Ostrich plumes differ
From chicken feathers (p. 53)

Explicitly, she never expresses any more specific judgement on the appearance of different racial groups but through the choice of animals in her later analogies a sourer note creeps in. It begins a few lines below the 'Ostrich plumes' when she compares Indian hair to 'the tail of a horse' and then white women's hair to 'That of the brown monkey' (p. 53). At the end of the section she is talking about black women wanting (or not wanting) to imitate other hair styles:

> . . . the crested crane
> Would hate to be changed
> Into the bold-headed,
> Dung-eating vulture.
> The long-necked and graceful giraffe
> Cannot become a monkey. (p. 63)

The derogatory impressions of 'vulture' and 'monkey' are balanced by the 'crested crane' and 'giraffe' with their very precise suggestion of the long poised neck Lawino describes in the middle of the section, unhidden by hair, straight as the 'alwiri spear', its graceful lines further extended by the long-necked jar balanced on the woman's head.

'Song of Malaya' is apparently addressed to the urban sector of society in which the imported norms of sexual morality have now won official acceptance. The attitude to polygamy and promiscuity preached by the bishop is also taught to the malaya's son in school; it is the cause of her brother's shame at her occupation, it encourages the attitude of the jealous wives, and it is given legal expression in the occasional police operations like the one which traps the malaya at the end of the poem. The malaya is therefore attacking accepted social norms rather than advocating adherence to those norms, and this tends to make her satire more biting than that of oral songs or Okot's earlier poems. The malaya aims to show the folly of the official morality by proving that no one actually follows it and she does this by exposing the guilty secrets of her enemies. The nearest parallel to this in oral songs is the attack on the chiefs who become the servants of the British administration, like the song against the 'gossiper chief', Chief Olal who reported his subjects to the DC. (See above, p. 89) The singers of that *bwola* song are attacking the new colonial administration by making public their chief's secret activities. The malaya lampoons her brother by broadcasting the details of his noisy visit to a prostitute's hotel (pp. 176–7); she reminds the schoolteacher of his activities amongst his girl pupils (p. 173), she drags up the bishop's dubious parentage to undermine his preaching (p. 161), and announces to the World at large the Big Chief's impotence on his drunken visit to her (p. 136).

The next song, an *otole* song of the Pajule chiefdom, recalls a time when the whole chiefdom had fled westwards across the river Acaa because of a severe famine. Their chief, dissatisfied with his position as a guest of others rather than the leader of his own people, tried to persuade them to leave their hosts and return eastwards. The memory of famine was still strong in their minds and there was no certainty that they would not meet hardship again if they returned. The situation is dramatized by this bitter reply to the chief:

Kong i ciom ma i lalur
Ki ma oto i pii
Ka dok inyut dero bel
Ka wek wadok malo
Wan pud wacamo lumone

First you go and bring those entombed in the stomach of hyenas [who perished with hunger and were eaten by hyenas]
And those who died in rivers [because too weak to swim across River Acaa]
And then you show millet granaries [from which supplies will be obtained]
And then we shall return to the East
We are still eating sweet potatoes [from Bantu *lumonde*, introduced into Acoli recently from Bunyoro and for some time only to be found in West Acoli]
('Oral Literature Among the Acoli and Lang'o', p. 66.)[4]

The last line, in particular, is a very subtle epigrammatic answer to the chief. It is in the present tense: where they are there is enough food and so they are still eating, but their humble role as guests depending on charity is suggested by the contrast between '*bel*' (millet) and '*lumone*' (sweet potatoes). It implies the singer's despair of finding food if he returns to the East now and also his defiance for the future: he will carry on eating '*lumone*' until the dead return to life and he hears of the millet granaries full awaiting his return home. This sardonic tone occurs in Okot's writing in the 'Song of a cripple', the words of the beggar in *Song of Ocol* who is in many ways the direct ancestor of the vagrant (see below, p. 122), and in 'Song of Prisoner' itself. The methods of this 'Song' are far from those of satirists who believe that social health is achievable. They belong to what Northrop Frye calls the 'sixth phase' of satire which 'presents human life in terms of largely unrelieved bondage': 'Song of Prisoner' is a 'nightmare of social tyranny' (*Anatomy of Criticism*, p. 238). The prisoners do not lampoon, their attacks on others are always expressions of their despair and self-pity as in the vagrant's attacks on his own parents and his appeal to his old employer to let him forget his past activities as a bodyguard (p. 117). The poem piles pictures of destruction of human and animal life on top of one another to convey the impression of a whole society trapped in a prison of mutual violence.

The *lucak wer* may be an unaffected observer, detached from and untouched by, the fault he ridicules, as in the song about the girl who cannot 'do the *teke*' (see above, p. 90), he may be a spokesman for an affected group as in the song against Chief Olal, the informer chief (see above, p. 89), or he may be more personally involved as is probably the case in the songs against the inheritor, where his rivalry for the inheritance may well lie behind his song. He rarely sings in the tone of intense personal grievance that motivates

Lawino and the prisoner and to a lesser extent Ocol and the malaya. The women's songs '*Abedo mera ataa*' and '*Wan mon walony ku*' (see above, pp. 27–8) do have this tone of grievance; they are very close to *Song of Lawino* in their methods of defence and counterattack on errant husbands:

Ojengo lela,
Lwonga, aye,
Cwara yeto maa,
Ayela pa co,
Rac araca ki wor;
Okako kongo, oyeng,
Ngok i koma;
Walony awene?

He stands his bicycle,
He calls me, I respond,
My man hurls insults at my mother;
The troubles of men are ceaseless,
At night they are worse.
He drinks to his full,
And vomits on me;
When shall we have peace?
(*Horn of My Love*, p. 60)

The dramatic interest of Okot's 'Songs' arises out of the feeling of personal grievance within them. Because of the singer's dispute with those he lampoons, the emphasis of the poems shifts from the follies of the singer's victim to an interest in the conflict between singer and victim.

This technique is not unknown in oral songs. The *lucak wer* usually sing in their own voices, but they sometimes dramatize a situation by assuming a fictional voice, as in these two songs of the Paimol chiefdom. On one occasion this chiefdom was attacked by an alliance of Arabs and the chiefdom of Kabala because of its failure to provide a tribute to the Arab slave traders. The Paimol were defeated. When the protection of the Arabs was withdrawn, the Paimol, in alliance with the Pa-Cua, conducted a vengeance raid on Kabala's chiefdom. This *bwola* song justifies the vengeance raid and the singer assumes the voice of a mother whose son was killed in the first battle to dramatize the situation:

Oneko woda ye,
Jo pa Onyang obutu i tim;
Ee, ngwec oloyo ya Kabala.
Onyang yang ajuki kwe;
Ngwec oloyo kitino pa Onyang . . .

The enemy killed my son;
Now the sons of Onyang are scattered in the wilderness;
Ee, the people of Kabala could not escape
Onyang, I did advise you, but you refused;
Now the sons of Onyang are scattered in the wilderness;
(*Horn of My Love*, p. 166)

The range of this battle was increased when a man of the Patongo chiefdom was killed by the Paimol in one of their raids on Kabala. The Patongo killed some women of the Paimol chiefdom because of this death and then themselves suffered a vengeance raid from the Paimol. The element of dramatic projection is here greater in that the Paimol *otole* song below is sung in the voice of a timid Patongo warrior appealing to his general, Rungula Nyepur, not to start a feud with the Paimol by killing the Paimol women:

Rungula Nyepur tero wa do i to;
Rungula, woda dong i nguny tugu.
Gwok ier ali wa ya.
Rungula woda dong in ngony tugu;
Ii, Akwang ma lakee.

Rungula Nyepur leads us to our death;
Rungula, my son will die under the barusus palm;
Do not start a feud,
Rungula, my son will die under the barusus palm;
The spirit Akwang demands human sacrifice.
(loc. cit)

This song celebrates the ferocity of the Paimol by satirizing the cowardice of the Patongo. The character whose voice the satirist assumes is the 'butt' rather than the 'mouthpiece' of his satire.

Lawino, Ocol, and the malaya are each to some extent mouthpieces of Okot's satirical purposes: their lampoons and general satirical attacks express comments on society which are Okot's own. The prisoners are rarely mouthpieces because their attacks on others always illuminate their own predicament more effectively than they comment on others. Lawino, Ocol, and the prisoners are also butts of Okot's satire: as fictional characters they represent particular aspects of the society he is commenting upon. The weakness of the fiction in 'Song of Malaya' (see above, p. 66) is such that the malaya is never a butt of Okot's satire; she does not validly represent the predicament or attitudes of any social group. Her mood of exaltation in the face not only of all kinds of abuse but even of arrest and eternal damnation (p. 183) is utterly implausible. Oculi's Rosa battling against boredom and despair is much closer to the social reality of prostitution in contemporary Africa. The singers' roles as butts of Okot's satire are discussed in the next chapter against the background of the problems of Acoli society they represent, and their roles as mouthpieces are discussed in Chapter 8 in relation to Okot's opinions as expressed in his academic work.

Notes to Chapter 6

1. For a discussion of realism in the modern European novel, see Wayne C. Booth, *The Rhetoric of Fiction*, Chicago: The University of Chicago Press, 1961, ch. 2, pp. 23–64.
2. Ruth Finnegan challenges 'The idea that African stories are above all designed to convey morals' and suggests that 'within a culture stories are likely to have many functions', *Oral Literature in Africa* p. 377. Okot's account of the manner of adult story telling seems to confirm her point of view in relation to the Acoli.
3. The songs about soldiers discussed in Chapter 8 (below, pp. 142–5) deal with similar conflicts in similar ways.
4. The translation given in the version published in *Horn of My Love*, p. 156, is much freer and, though it reads better, it misses some of the wit of the original.

7 'Lok pa Lukwan'

GULLIVER, in so far as he is the butt of Swift's satire, represents the whole of the satirized society in his naïve defence of some of the customs attacked by those he meets on his voyages. He therefore appears in each of the four voyages to lands of fantasy which both represent and contrast with the satirized society, Okot's singers represent different parts of the society and are placed in a slightly overstated version of the real situation to give us conflicting view of the same social reality. In his book on satire, Arthur Pollard notes that the satiric character

> ... can possess only a limited independence. More than most fictional characters he is the creature of his maker. No matter what he is in himself, he always remains the creature of his master's satiric intention.
> (Arthur Pollard, *Satire*, p. 54)

The limitations of Okot's singers seen as individuals (see above, pp. 67–83). arise from the control exercised over them by their function in Okot's satire Arthur Pollard continues:

> The satiric position is defined early in a work and the character serves to illustrate it. He does not become; he is. He does not develop, or if he does, he may ... outgrow his creator's original purpose.
> (loc. cit.)

Of Okot's characters only Lawino develops from her role in the satirical scheme into a nearly plausible individual and in doing so outgrows Okot's original purpose. This aspect of *Song of Lawino* enriches the poem and does not in the least detract from her function as a representative character but it is a false signpost to Okot's methods as a poet. In criticizing *Song of Lawino* because the characters are not 'real people' but 'caricatures', Ali Mazrui and Okumo pa'Lukobo have followed the false signpost and judged the poem by the wrong set of standards. Ali Mazrui's final assertion that Ocol 'could in no way be regarded as representative of the type of person he wants to typify' (see above, p. 72) does not follow from the fact that Ocol is a caricature. Lawino, Ocol, and the prisoners do represent the predicament and many of the attitudes of certain social groups in recent Ugandan history.

In his essay 'Okot p'Bitek and Writing in East Africa', Ngugi wa Thiong'o points this out and also notes the representative nature of the portrayal of Lawino:

> A few critics have reacted against what they see as her jealousy-motivated defence of every aspect of tradition. They thus turn the fundamental opposition between two value-systems into a mere personal quarrel between Lawino and her husband. We must in fact see the class basis of her attack: Lawino is the voice of the peasantry and her ridicule and scorn is aimed at the class basis of Ocol's behaviour.
> (Ngugi wa Thiong'o, *Homecoming*, p. 75)

All Okot's literary works are concerned with a very specific social process: the emergence and subsequent development of a parody of a Western-style class structure within African societies; and a full appreciation of them depends on an understanding of the historical background of this process. Folk tales centre on the family group. To understand them would involve a study of the life within that group. The *orak* songs cover a slightly wider community and are tied to lampooning those within that community. Okot's 'Songs' spread their satirical subject a little more widely, but *Song of Lawino* and *Song of Ocol* primarily represent the experience of Acoliland and are relevant elsewhere only by analogy. Okot's poems are rightly discussed generally in a pan-African context as the social process they describe has taken place with variations in many parts of the continent, but they represent pan-African problems through the microcosm of a particular community.

The people who live in the present administrative districts of East and West Acoli are descendants of some of the groups who were involved in the large-scale Luo migrations a few centuries ago. These major movements of people were probably complete before the end of the eighteenth century although there was no shortage of uncultivated land in the Acoli area and the splitting of clans and migrations of newly formed clans within the area have continued, as is illustrated by Okot's accounts of migrations within his own (Pa-Cua) clan (*Religion of the Central Luo*, pp. 88 and 89). The people in the area are linked by language and culture with other Luo groups, and the majority of them are also racially Luos, but there is a racial mixture; they have absorbed non-Luos they found on their arrival in their present area and other non-Luo groups who came later and sought the protection of a particular chief (J. K. Girling, *The Acholi of Uganda*, p. 13). The name 'Acoli' is a corruption of the word 'Shuli' first used by the Arabs in the nineteenth century and later adopted by other invaders. The people previously called themselves Luo, as did their neighbours, the Alur in the west and the Jo-pa-Luo of Kibanda in the south. Okot argues that the Acoli had no sense of ethnic solidarity as a group distinct from their Luo neighbours until the myth of 'tribes', used as a basis of administration by the colonial government, created that feeling (*Religion of the Central Luo*, pp. 1–8). There were certainly no centralized institutions to identify Acoliland as a political entity.

The concept of the family was central to all social organization in the area before the coming of the Arabs in the nineteenth century. The most important unit of social obligation was the clan. Clans usually occupied a particular area which would be closed for protection against outsiders but their defining characteristic was the claim of all members of each clan to be descendants of a particular man. Each clan had its own hunting area, organized communal work on clan common land, had its own ancestral shrine with its own lineage elder, the ritual authority within the clan, and arranged *orak* dances. Clans were often suspicious of, or openly hostile to, their neighbours, and they were continually spawning new clans when a particular family felt strong enough to move and settle in a new area. The head of the family would become the new lineage head, from whom all members claimed descent. The only larger unit of organization was the chiefdom under the *rwot*. There were about thirty different chiefdoms of varying size in Acoliland on the arrival of the British administration (Colin Leys, *Politicians and Policies*, p. 16). Each chiefdom consisted of two groups of clans, one *lokal* claiming a blood relationship with the *rwot*, and the other, the commoner group, making no such claim, although the system was flexible as famine or war might rob a particular clan of its *lokal* status. All clans paid tributes to the *rwot* and sought his help in settling disputes with other clans or his protection against an external enemy, and each chiefdom could trace its history through the genealogy of the royal family back to the beginnings of the chiefdom and, in some cases, to the mythical origins of the Luo people.

The word *won* (father or owner) is used to express lordship at every level of organization from *won-wa* (our owner), the head of every household, to *won ngom* (owner of the land) which was one title for the *rwot*. The myth explaining how the title of 'owner of the land' originated, which represents 'the first king in the world' as a lame man, the weakest of a group of brothers,[1] seems to suggest that he was expected to be wise rather than strong. The title did not give him arbitrary power; it entitled him to a rent in labour or kind from every clan in the chiefdom in return for the political duties of settling disputes within the chiefdom and organizing war against external enemies. The *rwot* was also ritual head of the chiefdom with important functions connected with the annual feast at the chiefdom shrine (*Religion of the Central Luo*, pp. 59–85). The *rwot* held his position only by the consent of the clans as the laws of succession to the office were not universally applied. One son could be preferred over another by the support of the clans and there were frequent changes of lineage in smaller chiefdoms whilst disputes over the succession were common in larger ones. Chiefdoms showed the same tendency to fragment and spawn new ones as clans, disputes over the succession being more often settled by splitting the chiefdom than by fighting for the office of *rwot*.[2]

Thus the Arab slave traders who began to operate in Acoliland in the 1820s (*Religion of the Central Luo*, p. 135), attracted by the area's potential as a source of the lucrative commodities of ivory and slaves, found a highly fragmented political organization which was slow-moving and based on consent and therefore unable quickly to organize strong resistance to them. European 'explorers' passed through Acoliland in their search for the source of the Nile and their accounts of the slave trade persuaded the Egyptian government to try to administer the area as part of Equatoria Province with the aim of tapping the profits of the ivory trade and suppressing the slave trade. Sir Samuel Baker's term as ruler of the province from 1871 to 1873 was popular with the Acoli and he seems to have tackled the slave traders with some success, but he employed some former slave traders as his soldiers and, after his departure, the trade was resumed with renewed vigour (J. Milner Gray, 'Acoli History 1860–1901, Part 1', pp. 123–40). Because Equatoria was a very large province, neither Gordon nor Emin Pasha, the later rulers, was able to control his subordinates. Emin spent only a small proportion of his time in Acoliland, and, in his absence, his subordinates continued to extort from the Acoli quantities of grain far in excess of the tax that Baker had initiated. In 1881, the Mahdist uprising in the north of Equatoria Province cut Emin's line of communication northwards and left him a prey to the increasingly organized hostility of the Acoli to him and his Arab troops. Okot records the involvement of his Pa-Cua ancestors, Lalwak and Keny Koropil, in the battle of Akworo between an alliance of chiefdoms including the Payira and Patiko and the Arabs (*Religion of the Central Luo*, pp. 88–9 and 136). The combined effects of the continuing Mahdi revolt and the fighting in Acoliland led Emin Pasha to leave the area in a relief column led by Stanley which crossed Africa to the south of Acoliland and ended the attempt at Egyptian control of the area ('Acoli History 1860–1901, Part 1', pp. 123–40).

One group of Emin's troops remained in Acoliland and tried to maintain control of a strip of land from Dufile to Wadelai to the east of the Nile, but they were small units of aliens in a hostile country, unable to venture far outside their fortresses without strong military escort and living off the products of occasional looting raids on the countryside (J. Milner Gray, 'Acoli History 1860–1901, Part 2', p. 32). This escalating process of violence and counter-violence was now made worse by Swahili gunrunners, and slave traders operating from Mombasa whose activities made a gun a necessary item in a household as a means of self-defence against a possible raid from them, usually operating in alliance with a near-by hostile clan or chiefdom (A. B. Adimola, 'The Lamogi Rebellion, 1911–12, pp. 167 and 169). Military campaigns northwards from the new Uganda Protectorate from 1898 to 1901 led to the isolation and defeat of remaining Arab groups and the beginning of theoretical British control in Acoliland, but no effective administration was established as the economically poor north of Uganda was not considered worth the expense. In the absence of any strong authority, Swahili traders continued their activities until the colonial government was eventually persuaded of the need for administration in the north and further military campaigns from 1910 to 1913 paved the way for this (J. P. Barber, 'The Moving Frontier of British Imperialism in Northern Uganda', pp. 27–41).

The half-century of looting and raiding by competing groups of powerful outsiders drastically impoverished Acoliland, involving slaughter of cattle and destruction of crops on an unprecedented scale. It also led to either the weakening, or the distortion into something new, of the institution of the *rwot*. At first the *rwodi* were unable to provide protection for the clans under them, but after 1880 some of them began to imitate the military methods of the Arabs. The chief's enclosure of Rwot Iburaim Awic of Payira held a permanent body of men with guns for defensive purposes and he also established a system of small chieftainships among the Payira clans, each with its own group of armed men, who could be quickly mobilized for battle. Because of his adoption of these methods he was widely respected in Acoliland and was probably the most powerful man in the area during the late 1890s (Reuben S. Anywar, 'The Life of Rwot Iburaim Awic', p. 72). Other *rwodi* sought the protection of a strong outsider against the raids of their neighbours and no group was strong enough to be independent of short-lived and unreliable alliances and so no chiefdom could give security and stability to the clans within it. There was an atmosphere of mistrust and fear throughout the country and a state of nearly continuous war between Arabs, Swahili alliances of chiefdoms, and any invading British force in the area (J. Milner Gray, 'Acoli History 1860–1901, Part 3', pp. 132–41).

The distortion of the office of the *rwot* was given a new twist with the arrival of the British administration in 1913. Administrators moved up from Kampala, where the colonial government had used agents of the feudal Baganda Kingdom as civil servants in the new protectorate. They looked for local agents of their centralized authority in northern Uganda, trying to apply the Baganda model of political authority in radically different conditions. The *rwodi* seemed to be the natural people to undertake these new jobs, but, as they were being asked to exercise arbitrary authority in a way they had never done before, many of them failed, some simply reporting that their people would not obey them. Many of them were therefore dismissed and new chiefs, often from a completely different area, were appointed on the judgement of their superior officers (J. P. Barber, 'The Moving Frontier of British Imperialism in Northern Uganda', pp. 36–8). Thus the connection between lineage and political function was destroyed as the new government-appointed chiefs took over the functions associated with the title *won ngom* by collecting taxes and dealing with disputes about the ownership of land (D. O. Ocheng, 'Land Tenure in Acoli', *Uganda Journal*, vol. XIX, no. 1, March 1955, pp. 60–1). The lineage of the *rwot* retained its ritual functions but these declined in importance with the decline of the annual feast at the chiefdom shrine (*Religion of the Central Luo*, p. 17). In the first few years of the system there were many anti-chief riots in various parts of Acoliland but, after 1920, the change was reluctantly accepted (J. P. Barber, 'The Moving Frontier of British Imperialism in Northern Uganda', pp. 36–8), although the *bwola* and *otole* songs against chiefs indicate the radical change of attitude to them caused by their use by the British administration. Most Acoli are still aware of the traditional chiefdom to which they belong and owe it some loyalty (Colin Leys, *Politicians amd Policies*, p. 16).

The old flexible system of political authority and social organization, marked by government by consent and small distinctions in wealth, began to be replaced by a new system of authoritarian and centralized government with vast distinctions in wealth. The colonial government and the missionaries were the joint agencies in the creation of the new system. As a result of his refusal to agree to the demands of British invaders during their campaigns after 1898, Rwot Iburaim Awic was imprisoned in Kampala from 1901 to 1902 (Reuben S. Anywar, 'The Life of Rwot Iburaim Awic', p. 76). On his return from imprisonment he was full of news of *Muni-kwan* (the white men of reading—the missionaries) who were revealing the white men's secrets to people in other parts of Uganda, but not to the Acoli. With the adaptability that he had already shown in his fortress techniques of battle, he saw the possibilities in taking the white men's secrets on other subjects for use in his own way and invited the teachers from a mission in Bunyoro into his chiefdom. In 1904 an *ot kwan* (reading house) was established and chiefs from all over Acoliland were invited to send two sons to receive instruction in reading, arithmetic, and the catechism. The 'reading house' remained in existence until 1908, when an obscure incident led to conflict between the teachers and their hosts and the hasty departure of the missionaries (J. K. Russell, *Men Without God?*, pp. 19–25). A few people still continued their reading and an *ot kwan* was re-established in 1910. A permanent CMS mission station was set up in Gulu in 1913, about the same time as the Catholic Verona Fathers, moving south from the Sudan, also began their missionary activities. In the new conditions of the British administration there was a period of very rapid expansion for the missionaries. The CMS station started with a staff of five teachers, all working in Gulu, but within four or five years it had teachers all over Acoliland, so that a second major mission could be established at Kitgum in 1917. The expansion continued during the 1920s and 1930s. A group of elders in a particular place would hear about the missionaries and request their own *ot kwan*; they would build a hut to serve as both church and school and an ill-qualified teacher would be sent to them (ibid., pp. 26–32).

The missionaries were laying the seeds of two areas of social conflict whose full destructive force did not become evident until the 1850s and 1960s. Firstly there was the conflict between the 'educated', who had access to steadily higher ranks of political power, and the 'uneducated', who did not understand, and were prevented from participating in, the new political system; and secondly there was the division between the two groups of converts, the Catholics and the Protestants. The Verona Fathers and the CMS missionaries began work in Acoliland at roughly the same time and entered into vigorous competition to satisfy the enthusiasm for the new learning. In some parts of Africa competing missions arrived at a *modus vivendi* by establishing different denominations in different areas, but in Acoliland there was no such compromise. In every part of the area, CMS and Catholic *ot kwan* were established side by side. Evidence of this wasteful absurdity still survives in the presence of two primary schools, often both half-empty, very close to each other in many villages in Acoliland. The two groups of converts were implacably hostile to each other and had a new basis of allegiance which could cut across chiefdom, clan, and even household loyalties.

At first, though, Christianity had little effect on people's social behaviour. Learning in the *ot kwan* provided a means to political power and to the mastery of the white man's technology and these areas of existence did not impinge on clan and household rituals which cemented together the lives of the majority of the Acoli. In the early records of the CMS church in Gulu there is no evidence that there was any conflict over church membership and attendance at clan rituals; such an issue was never discussed by the Church Council. Bishop J. K. Russell concludes that clan rituals have been affected hardly at all by missionary activity:

> Probably 90% of the homes in Acoli still have connection with clan ritual at times of need. . . . This means that if Christianity in its early days in Acoli did replace clan ritual, then there has been a massive reversal over the years. It seems more likely that the clan ritual has never been displaced: it has always held, and still holds, its central position in the life of the Acoli people.
> (ibid., pp. 28–9)

Many converts continued to take part in clan rituals, as is illustrated by the cases of dismissed teachers who have become local chiefs and experts on clan ritual whilst still retaining church membership (loc. cit.). Okot illustrates the continuing clan loyalties of Christians in relation to his father with the tale of how in 1938, fourteen years after he had gone to Gulu, he could be called in the middle of the night to go the fifteen miles to Ajulu to fight for the clan when it was in trouble (*Religion of the Central Luo*, pp. 88–9). After his father's death in 1971, the *guru lyel* ceremony was performed at Ajulu.[3]

Acoliland was too hot, disease-ridden, and dry for European settlers and none of the crops in the area was suitable for export. The main change to agriculture in the area during the colonial period was the introduction of cotton. In many parts of Acoliland each clan or household had its own small acreage of cotton alongside the food crops grown for its own consumption. This provided the marginal cash subsidy needed for taxes and school fees in what remained largely a subsistence economy. For the large numbers of people whose crops had been frequently destroyed and whose stocks of cattle had been depleted or wiped out by the half-century of looting, the only way out of the spiral of poverty was to get a salaried job, as the lowest-paid salaried job would give more wealth than one could expect to get from cotton. As the colonial government continued to concentrate its attention on the fertile centre of Uganda, there were very few opportunities for work within Acoliland and so the young Acoli man was forced to travel. It was these pressures which persuaded many Acoli to join the much-satirized ranks fighting the 'white man's battles' (see below pp. 142–5), first in Burma during the Second World War and then in the King's African Rifles in Kenya during the emergency in the early 1950s. The Acoli continued to be numerous in the colonial and then the Ugandan army as well as the police until Amin's massacres of them in August 1971 and thereafter.

In the 1940s and 1950s, the army and police provided secure employment for a large number of Acoli, but there were not enough opportunities for all those in need. From those who travelled in search of other jobs and failed to find them, came first the trickle and then the flood of the urban poor, the lumpenproletariat, that Frantz Fanon describes:

> The landless peasants who make up the lumpenproletariat, leave the country districts, where vital statistics are just so many insoluble problems, rush towards the towns, crowd into tin-shack settlements, and try to make their way into the ports and cities founded by colonial domination.
> (Frantz Fanon, *The Wretched of the Earth*, p. 88)

Okeca Ladwong, the hero of Okot's Acoli novel *Lak Tar*, is a representative of the victims of that spiral of poverty as it affected the Acoli in the 1950s. The title of the novel itself suggests his poverty; it is taken from Okeca's father's nickname, which was the proverb '*Lak tar miyo kinyero wi lobo*' (Our teeth are white, that is why we laugh at the sorrows of the world; *Lak Tar*, p. 1). People who think that Okeca Ladwong laughs because he is happy are mistaken, he laughs only because of that proverb which tells him that 'Sadness and sorrow should not weigh us down. ('Oral Literature Among the Acoli and Lang'o', p. 372). His father dies while he is still young enough to be herding goats and he and his mother and sister unwillingly become part of his uncle's household. He only begins to discover the real extent of his problems when he needs to raise money for the bride price. Cecilia, the girl he falls in love with, gives him a love token of beads which indicates acceptance of him but also intimates that she expects a bride price of 1,000 shillings. Okeca's approach to his stepfather is rebuffed with a long tale of the stepfather's financial woes, and approaches to other relatives raise only fifty shillings. Apart from going away to work, his only choice is to wait for the marriage of his sister for her bride price to pay his. Even this is unlikely to work because his sister is both uneducated and unattractive and therefore unlikely to raise a large bride price.

He looks into the pay for work in Acoliland, but concludes it would take him ten years to raise the money. Only Kampala wages might help him, but when he goes to Kampala, he finds that, though there are well-paid jobs, there are too many people like him who want them. After an uncomfortable period in Kampala living in very crowded conditions with a family of distant relatives who make it clear he is unwelcome, he obtains unpleasant but well-paid work in Jinja sugar plantations. Workers on the plantation are bonded to stay for five years; Okeca works well and is promoted to easier work, but his good luck breaks. He uses a forged letter to help a friend to break his bond and escape home before five years are up. His accomplice in this betrays him and he is demoted again to heavy work. Though he has not raised the money he needs, this is too much for him and he too escapes and makes his way home. In the confusion at Kampala bus station both his luggage and his money are stolen and he cannot even afford the bus fare for the last stage of his journey, but has to walk home as poor and miserable as ever.

This plot holds together a satirical commentary on many aspects of life in Acoliland. A good part of Chapter 1, for example, is taken up with a description of Okeca's meeting as a child with an uncle who was an army officer, though this has no relevance to the plot. The army officer is mocked for his boasts about his travels to a young boy and the mixture of Acoli and Swahili that he speaks (ibid., pp. 3–5). Chapter 2 occupies fourteen pages and its contribution to the plot is the description of the first two meetings between Okeca and Cecilia, one of which takes two pages and the other about three pages. The remainder of the chapter is taken up with descriptions of the events at which the meetings take place, a Saturday market and a wedding *orak* dance. Okeca's wooing is direct and without preliminaries as it should be according to Okot's essay on Acoli love (*Africa's Cultural Revolution*, p. 48). A group of young men meet a line of girls and Okeca picks out his girl Cecilia, 'shooting' her with the cry '*Rip kipi*', which imitates the sound of a gun, and then immediately making his proposal:

> *Nye, nya pa mara, an amiti matek tutwal, amito ni in kikomi aye ibibedo dako agit mera; itamo nining? An adegi.*
> (*Lak Tar*, p. 15).
>
> [Hallo, daughter of my mother-in-law, I want you very strongly, I really want only you to become my wife; what do you think?
> I don't want you.]

Okeca continues to plead his case and Cecilia rejects him in accordance with the etiquette of a first meeting (*Africa's Cultural Revolution*, p. 48), but while they are still in the midst of the argument Okeca describes the scene around them. The market is crowded and dirty; you have to be careful when you go there and it is best to walk in groups. He gives us snatches of the conversations you hear as you walk; women gossiping, criticizing their husbands, a man trying to make an arrangement to meet a woman in her home and a well-travelled man showing off.

After Chapter 3, when Okeca's troubles begin to gather momentum, he becomes an innocent abroad, the victim at every point of those who fail to live up to the conventional norms of his society in their treatment of him. All his troubles stem from the absurdly inflated bride price that Cecilia's father is asking of him, and Okot underlines the point that this is not unusual by showing us many other young men who are in the same position as Okeca. On buses, in prison, and especially when working in Jinja, Okeca meets young men like himself, who have been forced to leave Acoliland in the prime of their lives because they wanted to get married. It is the duty of Okeca's uncle to help him out of his troubles and treat him in the same way as he treats his own son and, his relatives in Kampala should receive him warmly and help him willingly until he can find the work that he wants, but instead their rudeness helps to drive him to Jinja. In Jinja, again, an Acoli, his fellow conspirator in the help that they give to someone else, betrays him. In Okeca Ladwong's rural community the new class structure has not yet emerged but the process of its creation has begun and is moving apace. Already, in 1953, a good schooling is the key to a good marriage and it is the wealthy, 'educated' people who have caused the bride price to be inflated. Every girl now wants to marry an 'educated' man: in Jinja, when Okeca is beginning to plan his friend's escape, they discuss the girls they used to know who have become proud because they want 'educated' boys:

> *Lok pa lukwan kono tye marac mada paco kwica. Pien wa anyira ma pe gingeyo wa 'A' bene gito pi awobe Makerere.*
> (*Lak Tar*, p. 108)
>
> [This business of 'educated' people is very bad at home there. Because even girls that don't even know 'A' also die for Makerere boys.]

This '*lok pa lukwan*' (business of educated people) is the root of the division between the peasant Lawino and the prisoner of the lumpenproletariat on the one hand, and Ocol on the other.

One effect of the travels of those Acoli young men who found secure jobs was to make them much more politically conscious than their counterparts in neighbouring districts. Their experiences in Burma and Kenya especially made them aware of the international nature of anti-colonial activities so that when the political parties emerged in the 1950s this well-travelled group was very ripe ground for them. The Uganda National Congress was founded in Buganda in 1952 and quickly spread to other areas of Uganda, including Acoliland. It was a radical party, opposing abuses of chiefly power like compulsory labour and arbitrary punishment but, among the Acoli, it was quickly seen as the beginnings of an independence movement (Colin Leys, *Politicians and Policies*, p. 17). Okot was one of the three men who began the organization of the Gulu branch of the UNC. He was very active in politics throughout the 1950s, being involved as a witness for the defence in the trial of the secretary general of the party in Acoliland and then, while in Britain in the years 1959 to 1961, helping in the organization of student support for the party, where he took part in meetings with Labour Party politicians to discuss how the process of bringing Independence could be speeded up. When the Independence elections were due in 1962 he considered becoming a candidate, but the party had already made arrangements for someone else to stand for the Gulu constituency, so Okot worked on his friend's election campaign whilst doing field work for his thesis. In 1971 he again considered standing as a parliamentary candidate but he decided not to and in any case the coup led to the suspension of political activities.[4]

Catholics throughout Uganda felt themselves to have suffered from half a century of British patronage of Protestants and the prospect of elections raised for them the possibility of bringing this to an end. Thus, in 1956, the Democratic Party was formed along the lines of the Christian Democratic parties of Europe as a party for Catholics and, because of the equality of size and the militancy of missionary groups in Acoliland, it naturally drew a lot of support there. The DP accused the UNC of Communism and the UNC in Acoliland saw the formation of the DP as an attempt by white priests to blunt the edge of their nationalist effort through the creation of a moderate party (Colin

Leys, *Politicians and Policies*, p. 18). Section 11 of *Song of Lawino* reflects these issues accurately: Ocol of the DP says that his brother 'will bring Communism!' and his brother says that the DP is 'the Party for Padres' and that its leaders 'hear everything from the Italian fathers' (p. 186). Britain began its colonial rule in Uganda by a treaty with the Kabaka of Buganda and within Buganda the Kabaka's privileges and authority were retained intact, whilst his influence spread outside his kingdom because of the favoured status he enjoyed within the Protectorate. To deal with the threat to his authoritarian position that the prospect of democracy raised, the Kabaka Yekka (Kabaka Only) Party was formed among the Baganda with the aim of preserving his power. To break the near-stalemate between the UNC and the DP, an alliance of the UNC and the Kabaka Yekka Party was formed, much to Okot's disgust,[5] and this alliance, dominated by the former UNC, now renamed the Uganda People's Congress, won the pre-Independence elections in 1962. In the local elections for the district council in Acoliland the UPC narrowly won, taking twenty-seven seats to the DP's twenty-three (Colin Leys, *Politicians and Policies*, p. 26).

Until the 1950s, local missionary schools gave only the kind of education needed for the smooth running of the colonial administration, creating a pool of people who understood the white man's ways well enough to work in local government but who had not travelled very far from their neighbours physically or culturally and shared in the continuing life of their clans, whatever privileges they might claim to bolster up their status. When the prospect of decolonization reared its head in the 1950s there began what Fanon called the 'rear-guard action' of the colonialists 'with regard to culture, values, techniques and so on' (Frantz Fanon, *The Wretched of the Earth*, p. 34). The colonial bourgeoisie sought to create and maintain close contact with a new black elite in their own image through the medium of vastly expanded opportunities for higher education in the metropolitan country. In 1953 there were only forty-seven students from Uganda studying abroad; by 1963 there were 1,656 (J. K. Russell, *Men Without God?*, p. 35). The minds of these people were set in a 'profoundly cosmopolitan mould' (Frantz Fanon, *The Wretched of the Earth*, p. 119) through their achievement of apparent equality of status with their colonial masters and of an appetite for the material paraphernalia of an urban environment. They were effectively alienated from their former neighbours in life style and in aspirations, yet when they returned they were given key positions in the political parties as they were the people with whom the colonialists were prepared to negotiate, and they therefore took over the higher reaches of power when Independence came.

Particularly in situations like that in Uganda, where Independence came without violence, the gulf that the experience of a European 'education' created between this new urbanized middle class and their former peasant neighbours was never bridged. Lacking any specific strategy for the transformation of their villages into a mechanized prosperity on the Western model, which was the only alternative they knew, and lacking even more any means of communicating the need for change or of mobilizing the rural community to work for change, they fell back on windy exhortations in their increasingly infrequent contact with rural communities. In his book *Politicians and Policies*, Colin Leys points out the gap in aspirations between these people and their constituents and the damage that this gap does to political activity. He says that

> . . . some party leaders are inclined to see all policy issues in the context of an overall transformation of society. . . . (p. 51).

Whilst, on the other hand,

> Acoli do not see politics as a way of revolutionizing life in the countryside; they see it rather as a way of improving, through government action, very many aspects of that life. Improving is not the same as transforming. (loc. cit.)

For the party leaders, improvements in government services are a means to stimulate changes in every aspect of life:

> . . . education will spread, consumption will rise but so will investment, productivity will go up, and so on; growth in each section of life will stimulate and be balanced by growth in all the others. . . .

Their constituents see things differently; for them,

> . . . government activity is seen as a dispenser of benefits, as a potential source of further income for individuals or groups . . . there is no general belief in a concept of social development. . . .
> (loc. cit.)

New wells, new roads, and new hospitals are desirable ends in themselves. They improve life by making it easier to live in the old ways.

Education is different, but even education does not represent a tool for transforming rural life, instead it provides 'the exit door from rural life' (loc. cit.). You do not expect your son to be a farmer when he has finished his schooling, you hope he will find a place for himself in the new corridors of power and shower down benefits on you and your clan. Out of this initial failure of communication between the political leader and the peasant communities springs the suspicion that Fanon describes:

> The disastrous experience of trying to enrol the country people as a whole reinforces their distrust and crystallizes their aggressiveness towards that section of the people.
> (Frantz Fanon, *The Wretched of the Earth*, p. 90).

The politicians keep away from the rural areas and become, as Lawino puts it:

> . . . rare
> Like the python
> With a bull water buck
> In its tummy (p. 195)

Instead of regaining contact with their clans, they remain true to the visions of a comfortable life that they gained from their student contact with Europe:

> We find intact in them the manners and forms of thought picked up during their association with the colonialist bourgeoisie. Spoilt children of yesterday's colonialism and of today's national governments, they organize the loot of whatever national resources exist.
> (Frantz Fanon, *The Wretched of the Earth*, p. 37)

Such corruption spreads to every aspect of political life. When government is seen as, at the very best, a haphazard patron giving away good things, it becomes a legitimate field for religious, clan, and chiefdom rivalry: its benefits are 'to be obtained by political manipulation in competition with other individuals and groups' (Colin Leys, *Politicians and Policies*, p. 51). The parties cling to what they have won, consolidate their power, and reward their followers. Thus, despite its very small majority, the UPC packed the committees of the district council with its own members (ibid., p. 27) and within the parties the old loyalties of chiefdom and clan come into play in the fight to divide the spoils of victory.

Section 11 of *Song of Lawino* accurately represents the kind of politics that results from this situation. At his political meetings Ocol makes no effort to communicate with his constituents about their immediate local problems; instead he 'reads . . . from a book' a collection of foreign slogans: 'Uhuru! Congress! Freedom!' and the crowds attend only for the festival atmosphere, the people they may meet there, and the dances which will follow (pp. 192–3). Lawino also sees the battles that go on behind this façade, most obviously between the two parties, where foreign slogans are again employed (p. 185), but also there is the battle within the party in the criticisms of other party leaders and the competition to please the men from Kampala (p. 191). These battles are both part of the struggle for the 'bull buffalo' of the new wealth available after Uhuru, in which there is only competition and no sharing, and in which the new form of strength is the ability 'to repeat empty lies' (p. 190). The result of these battles is the new and totally disruptive division throughout the country, creating the radically new situation within the community of 'the greatest wealth . . . surrounded by the greatest poverty' (Frantz Fanon, *The Wretched of the Earth*, p. 138):

> And those who have
> Fallen into things
> Throw themselves into soft beds
> But the hip bones of the voters
> Grow painful
> Sleeping on the same earth
> They slept
> Before Uhuru.
> (*Song of Lawino*, p. 195)

This, more than the violence, the interference, and the impositions of foreigners over nearly a hundred years, began to destroy the health of the clan basis of life within Acoliland and it is this spiritual ill-health that worries Lawino most of all. As Okeca was concerned about the evils that '*lok pa lukwan*' (the business of 'educated' people) had brought to the homestead, Lawino is concerned that 'the coming / Of the new political parties' has already caused the death of the homestead because 'the insides of the people are bad' with the hatred and envy implicit in this new class basis of social division within Acoliland (p. 197).

In his essay on *Song of Lawino*, 'Lawino is Inedu', Taban lo Liyong exempts Section 11 from his general condemnation of the poem:

> Chapter 11 is the only part written with enthusiasm. It is the only part of the book which has worth because it has relevance to the political games the Sons of Black have locked shoulders in.
> (*The Last Word*, p. 155)

He can justify the isolation of this section from the rest of the poem because of his insistence that it is 'newly added' (loc. cit.). One reason he gives for this assertion is his vague memory of the existence of the 1956 version of the poem which he calls 'Te Okono pe Luputu', which he may have seen and had certainly heard of in the 1950s, but did not have for comparative purposes when writing the essay. A poem written in 1956 could not possibly contain satire on the post-Independence politics of the early 1960s. This is true as far as it goes: Section 11 is a new addition, but so are Sections 8 and 9 and all the parts of the early sections which refer to Clementine. The 1966 poem is effectively a new poem (see above, pp. 33–6). The second justification is his biographical distinction between 'the Cultural Champion side of Okot' and 'the political side' (*The Last Word*, p. 138). This is valid in that Okot made two slightly half-hearted steps in the direction of a political career, which, if they had succeeded, would have considerably curtailed his activities as a champion of Acoli culture since the mid-sixties. However the contradiction between the aims of Okot's possible and actual career implied in sentences like: 'If the politician in him speaks, the social anthropologist keeps quiet' (loc. cit.) is not justified. It is impossible to judge whether Okot as a member of the political clique of the new bourgeoisie would have avoided the errors of judgement that the group made.

Taban's third reason for the isolation of Section 11, the small amount of support for this he draws from the text, ignores the emphasis in the section on the opposition of the values of family life to the politics of nationalism expressed through foreign slogans. Taban sees Okot's motives in the section as being the taking of personal revenge:

> . . . these . . . politicians frustrated Okot's chances of getting into Parliament. . . . And . . . the successful candidate in Okot's constituency is a DP member. It is likely that the DP is disparaged more than the UPC in this chapter because Okot was having his revenge.
> (loc. cit.)

The DP suffers marginally more than the UPC because Ocol is the DP candidate and is a much more important satirical butt than the 'brother', who makes only the one appearance in the poem, but the introduction and deflation of the brother generalizes the satire and directs it against all politicians. The section is certainly not a tactful manuscript for someone seeking a political future in either party. Taban draws no explicit link between this and his later, more telling comments on Okot's retention of missionary-induced prejudices against Catholics: 'Whenever he directs his barbs against the new religion, it is the Catholic catechist he is locked in unfair fight with' (ibid., p. 140). It is worthy of comment considering Okot's associations through his family with the CMS missionaries that the Protestants suffer only a little satire in the comment on the 'Labour to buy a name' (p. 113) that the missionaries exact from young converts and the accusation of cannibalism: 'O! protestants eat people!' (p. 115) to mock the communion service, whilst the Catholic church, which Okot knew much less about, is satirized by the long description of the Evening Speaker's Class (pp. 115–21) and the comments on the hypocrisy inherent in celibacy (p. 126). Similarly, having told us that both Catholics and Protestant priests hate questions, Lawino concentrates on the padre and the nun (p. 142), and it is Catholicism that suffers the small but sharp satirical barb about Ocol's use of charms through the mention of his crucifix, his daughter's rosaries, and the tale of the nun hugging her crucifix for protection against a snake (pp. 155–6). Having thus presented Ocol as a Catholic in Section 10, Okot must make him a DP member in Section 11.

In Section 11, however, Lawino's criticism is much more balanced; it is the whole paraphernalia of politics rather than the conduct or policies of either of the parties that bemuses and offends her. Her short criticisms of the propaganda of each of the parties are expressed on a commonsense level and are neatly paired: the UPC cannot 'remove all Catholics / From their jobs' (p. 186) since there are not enough Protestants to do the jobs; the DP cannot be controlled by white men, since white men are never seen at its public meetings (p. 187). Both comments naïvely take the exaggeration of party propaganda at its face value: Lawino doesn't understand the basis of division between the parties. The remainder of the section expresses a combination of incomprehension of the ways of politics and resentment of the disruption that politics has caused within the community she knows, especially within the family. Lawino's incomprehension is an indictment of both the parties; she is untouched by the most fundamental aspects of nationalism on which they both claim to be based; she confesses that she does not know the meaning of 'Uhuru', and innocently asks:

> And the Acoli and Lang'o
> And the Madi and Lugbara
> How can they unite?
> And all the tribes of Uganda
> How can they become one? (p. 188)

This indicates, in Fanon's terms, the failure 'to raise the standard of consciousness of the rank-and-file' (Frantz Fanon, *The Wretched of the Earth*, p. 108), the failure of the bourgeois leadership of both the nationalist parties to turn local grievances into a programme of political action. In the absence of any understanding of the idea of the national unit, Lawino sees politics only as a case of local disunity:

> Where is the Peace of Uhuru?
> Where is the unity of Independence?
> Must it not begin at home? (p. 188)

None of this is the vocabulary of one partisan politician taking revenge on others. For Okot, it was more likely to damage than aid his political future and it probably did contribute to the damage done to his political prospects as well as his other career by his removal from the Directorship of the Uganda National Theatre.

Taban's separation of 'culture' and 'politics' is unjustified, since Lawino's resentment of political activity springs from her central cultural concern, her anxiety for the continued health of the family. She begins by bewailing Ocol's extended absences from home during political campaigns, then turns to the more serious business of Ocol's enmity with his brother which prevents her talking to the man who may one day become her husband (p. 183), a worry to which she reverts at the end of the section in her fears for the damage the poison of hatred has done to the homestead. Throughout his essay Taban sees Lawino as a persona for Okot and his strongest objection is that she is a bad persona. He agrees that 'Lawino's song is commensurate with her comprehension and vision' (*The Last Word*, p. 155), but he fails to do justice to this vision and therefore dismisses the poem as 'light literature':

> Africans have been mad at expatriates for taking the African houseboy as the representative African. Okot hasn't done better by letting a mere catechist criticize the West and Westernization.
> (ibid., p. 141)

Lawino is not the representative African; she is better seen, as Ngugi suggested, as the voice of the peasantry, the representative African peasant and, as a mere catechist, she is uniquely qualified within contemporary African written literature to represent the African peasant because of the negligible nature of her exposure to 'the West and Westernization'. From this point of view even her implausible conservatism is of value, as it magnifies the issues just because it makes Lawino into 'a complete outsider' (see above, p. 72)—totally naïve before the Westernized aspects of her own society, like Gulliver thrust into each of the strange lands to which his voyages took him.

Similarly, Ocol's implausibility in the absence of nationalism from most of his pronouncements outside Section 11 (see above, pp. 72–4), though it is the one thing that gives some justification to Taban's separation of Section 11 from the rest of the poem, is of value because it gives a historical dimension to his present condition. Whether or not they are the same people, the political leaders who received their education abroad are in a direct line of descent from those enthusiastic converts who felt it necessary to express their intense loyalty to their new religion by the destruction of the symbols of the old. In their strange behaviour lay the seeds of the present unbridgeable gap in values and wealth between the bourgeoisie and the peasantry. When Ocol chased away the diviner priest from his father's homestead, 'People whistled in amazement' and wondered 'What ghost has captured / The head of Ocol?' (p. 158), but he was still sufficiently at one with the community to court

Lawino eagerly, despite his Christianity; and Lawino, for her part, 'used to admire him speaking in English' (p. 22). Then he went to Makerere and the white man's country and returned a total stranger, a man of power and a lover of new pleasures.

As an ultra-conservative 'outsider', Lawino is best able to point to the causes of his strange behaviour. Lacking the intellectual development of missionary conditioning, she can state bluntly that ballroom dancing is immoral because the dancers hold each other, and convincingly portray the sexuality of the traditional dance as a cleaner and sharper thing than the tobacco-laden constriction of the atmosphere in the ballroom where 'Men put their hands in the trouser-pockets' (p. 37). Because she has succumbed in virtually nothing to the fashion of imitation of the white man, she can point to the absurdity of dancing 'as white people do', of developing a taste for the tinned and processed foods of the white people, and attempting to imitate the cosmetics and the hair styles of white people. She can also point to the ultimate effect of this mimicry in Ocol's total loss of the dignity of manhood, first evidenced in the way that he 'runs from place to place / Like a small boy' (p. 95) in the pursuit of his incomprehensible business, then by his behaviour like 'a newly eloped girl' (p. 191) before the leaders of his party, but finally and most crucially clarified when he is described as 'A dog of the white man!' (p. 204).

In this respect *Song of Lawino* describes Ocol once again in terms which accord with Fanon's analysis. Fanon describes how 'because the national bourgeoisie identifies itself with the Western bourgeoisie from whom it has learnt its lessons', it becomes a pleasure-seeking group with no independence and no creative function, but only 'that of intermediary' between Western capitalism and the people of the new nation (Frantz Fanon, *The Wretched of the Earth*, pp. 122–3). As the white man's dog, Ocol is just such an intermediary, fierce in the protection of property but meek before his master:

> It chases away wild cats
> That come to steal the chicken!
> And when the master calls
> It folds its tails between the legs (p. 205)

He is grateful for whatever rewards come his way and protects his master well against any threat to his potential comfort:

> When the master is eating
> They lie by the door
> And keep guard
> While waiting for left-overs. (p. 205)

Grant Kamenju is therefore right to see Lawino's attempt in Section 13 to restore Ocol from this humiliation in terms of an attempted reclamation of the African bourgeoisie for a genuine nationalism looking to the peasant communities of Africa for its inspiration:

> Lawino's song is none other than the voice of the people—the black people—calling upon every enslaved Uncle Tom to abandon the role assigned him by imperialism of playing the lackey, the pimp and the zombie . . . it is an injunction to the black bourgeoisie who may still have eyes to see and ears to hear to join with the great mass of the African peasants and workers in the struggle against . . . imperialism and for the total liberation of black people everywhere.
> (Grant Kamenju, 'Black Aesthetics and Pan-African Emancipation', in Pio Zimiru and Andrew Gurr (eds.), *Black Aesthetics, Papers from a Colloquium held at the University of Nairobi, June* 1971, p. 193).

Song of Ocol indicates that Ocol did not have the ears to hear; for him, Lawino's song is a 'Song of the dead / Out of an old tomb' (p. 10), an echo of the past with no implications for the future.

Ocol in *Song of Ocol* is the politician of Section 11 of *Song of Lawino* without his campaigning masks. The phoney nationalism he displayed which amounted to the demand for 'the transfer into native hands of those unfair advantages which are a legacy of the colonial period' (Frantz Fanon, *The Wretched of the Earth*, p. 122) has disappeared now that the transfer of the town house and the big farm he boasts about (pp. 57–62) has been effected. Through his villainous self-revelations he confirms Fanon's and Lawino's analysis of the situation. The implausibility of this behaviour is again justified if the poem is taken in its satirical context as the voice of that petty-bourgeois clique that Lawino has been attacking. When the mask is off, Ocol willingly accepts his role as the heir to the colonial regime, wishing publicly to acknowledge his debt to Europe with statues and by eradicating images of the past (pp. 31 and 85) so as to ensure his continued acceptance as a true heir. Lacking any idea of the way to make useful technologies available to his people, he falls back on extravagant panegyrics of the potential might of technology which could fill the Rift Valley with rubble, and of the city he and his fellows will build (p. 84). Meanwhile he invites Lawino and her clansmen to leave their villages *en masse* and come to the existing city (pp. 78–80) but fails to mention the overcrowded shanty towns on its fringe.

He now treats these same clansmen with frank contempt, echoing the white man's racist vocabulary. They are 'Thoughtless and carefree / Like children dancing around a hut' (p. 56) and on his farm Ocol can wax lyrical about his 'prize bull' but has no place for 'natives':

When the tractor first snorted
On these hunting grounds
The natives scuttled into the earth
Like squirrels,
Like the edible rat
Pursued by the hunter's dog (pp. 60–1)

In Section 6 Ocol moves from distrust to aggressiveness against the peasantry. Having failed to mobilize them in the 'struggle for uhuru' Ocol now blames them for not contributing more (p. 56) and uses this as a justification for disclaiming responsibility for their social conditions (pp. 57–60). His description of his property leads his thoughts in the direction of fear of threats against it and causes him to bare his fangs with threats against trespassers and thieves until he comes to see the whole nation as a 'hunting ground' with himself and his friends in power as the hunters:

Have lions
Begun to eat grass,
To lie down with lambs
And to play games with antelopes?
Can a leopardess
Suckle a piglet? (p. 63)

Ocol has optimistically promoted himself from 'hunter's dog' for the white man to the role of hunter himself, but he has no qualms about the class society he has brought into existence and a very brutal class society it is where one class can confess that it feeds upon the other.

It turns out, however, that cornered 'natives' are more articulate and more dangerous than 'the edible rat'. The crippled beggar in Section 7 has an answer to the rhetorical question that Ocol asked near the beginning of Section 6:

What did you reap
When uhuru ripened
And was harvested? (p. 57)

At Uhuru those who had power, Ocol and his friends, sowed acres of the small seed of 'Cynicism' along with forests of 'Bitter Laughter'. The land was watered with the tears that the laughter provoked and the plants that grew throughout the new nation were 'Frustrations' with their ugly fruits 'Green as gall'. Alongside these 'Fear' was planted by the actions of Ocol and his friends, leaving 'festering wounds' unhealed on men's skins. In the midst of it lay 'Uhuru', a dead lamb, with the bourgeoisie like 'shimmering flies' giving it some appearance of life as they fed on the carcass. The 'herdsboy' who dared to throw small stones of criticism at the carcass was killed amidst the mocking laughter of those in power and his blood fertilized the land so that 'Cynicism' multiplied and a vast harvest was reaped. The cynicism was distilled like a spirit into anger which was trapped under pressure until one of those in power made the flash of fire that would cause the explosion:

> A hunter
> Sat in the shadow
> Of a rock,
> Rubbed two sticks
> A flash,
> Thunder roared,
> Flames
> Purified the Land! (pp. 65–70)

The crippled beggar has already been thrust out of the homestead—his prophecy of destruction is wider in its compass than that of Okeca and Lawino, as well as being more violent. It is his hope that destruction will engulf not, the homestead, but the bourgeois regime he is suffering under and that out of the violence will come a purification and a new beginning. In response to this threat, Ocol's petulant aggression reaches fever pitch as he abuses all those in the nation whom he believes do not deserve their freedom and drowns the beggar's words so that he still cannot hear.

The beggar's prediction came true in so far as the violence that has engulfed Uganda has swept away many members of that bourgeoisie who failed to take their opportunity in the early 1960s to be the creative leaders of their people, but this violence is not the revolutionary violence of the people but the violence of the military machine of the bourgeoisie now out of hand and devouring its own masters. It is far from clear whether such violence will ultimately 'purify' or poison the land; in the meantime the beggar's plant of 'fear' has the nation in its grip, as it has the 'singers' in Okot's 'Song of Prisoner'. After Independence, the illogical alliance between the UPC and the KY Party proved unworkable and broke down in 1964, when Obote felt strong enough to continue without it. In the atmosphere of political patronage already described, the opposition saw no way to break the stranglehold on power of the UPC without creating a crisis atmosphere in which force could be called in; and the Kabaka used rumours of an attempted coup as an excuse to call on the British army for help. Obote outmanoeuvred him and, because of the overwhelming strength of the northern communities in the army, managed to arrest the Kabaka; thereafter his government 'imposed armed rule throughout the Buganda countryside' (Colin Leys, *Politicians and Policies*,

p. 9) and depended increasingly on terror for its continued existence. It is this atmosphere that is reflected in Robert Serumaga's novel *Return to the Shadows*.

'Song of Prisoner' was published at about the time of Amin's coup, but was written before it. Although its dedication in both editions reflects a more consciously pan-African slant than that of the two 'Songs' published earlier, it describes most specifically the increasing dependence of Obote on thugs and torturers for his henchmen and, because of the accuracy of its picture of the atmosphere that preceded the coup, could be regarded as prophetic of the nature of Amin's regime. The festering wound of fear of a counter-coup in Amin's mind dashed the hopes of many that his coup, because of its non-violent start, could mark a creative turning point in Ugandan history. In particular, Amin exacted a heavy revenge for whatever benefits the Acoli within the army might have gained from Obote. As the largest potential power base fairly near in sympathy to Obote they were the first to suffer in the large-scale massacres of soldiers in August 1971, and Acoli within and outside the army have suffered repeatedly since. As Amin's paranoia has grown, his determination to eliminate all potential rivals has gained momentum and has included not only more and more groups within the army, but many others from among the bourgeoisie; and very many others have fled into exile. An alliance between those parts of the bourgeoisie and the peasants and workers of Uganda in the cause of a socially aware creative nationalism may now be possible, but the grip of the military on the country is strong and so far the exiled opposition has not found the means to break that grip.

The assassin and vagrant prisoners represent the same social type: the lumpenproletariat. Fanon described the lumpenproletariat as potentially the 'urban spearhead' of African revolution, 'the most spontaneous and the most radically revolutionary focus of a colonized people' (Frantz Fanon, *The Wretched of the Earth*, p. 103); it is perhaps because of this that both Atieno Odhiambo and Aloo Ojuka take the assassination in 'Song of Prisoner' to be a revolutionary act. Atieno Odhiambo tries to find a very specific reason for the poem's dedication to Patrice Lumumba, which he calls 'one of the most striking features' of the poem. He describes the importance of Lumumba's death in Africa 'because it was a killing allegedly executed by Africans . . . against . . . a leader of an African country *into independence*'. He goes on:

> The death of Lumumba dramatically spelt the beginning of the crumble of the mental edifice that the African had regarded as being the purpose of independence. The decade between the murder of Lumumba and the publication of 'Song of Prisoner' in 1971 saw the flowering of those tendencies, vestigal in the Congo in 1960–1, that were to be a negation of the intentions for independence.

Atieno Odhiambo, 'Two Songs, a Discussion, 1', in *Standpoints on African Literature*, pp. 100–2').

This seems to me reason enough for the dedication, but later he accepts the prisoner's evaluation of his own act as a heroic one and reminds us of the link with Lumumba: 'Just like Lumumba's life was a patriotic venture, so was the prisoner's act a patriotic assassination . . .' (ibid., p. 107). He then sees a contradiction implicit in this parallel he has just created, because the prisoner 'does not tell us what else there is to do . . .'. Aloo Ojuka modifies Atieno Odhiambo's view of the situation only in respect of the latter's insistent identification of 'the Prisoner' with 'the Intellectual'; he reminds us of the prisoner's poverty and the spontaneous nature (as he sees it) of the action, but still characterizes it as revolutionary: 'The prisoner has lit the revolutionary powder keg by murdering the mismanager. . . .' He sees in the prisoner's subsequent helplessness the request to educated Africans to 'come out and take over' the direction of the revolution (Aloo Ojuka, 'Two Songs, a Discussion, 2', in *Standpoints on African Literature*, pp. 122–4).

Neither of these views of the assassination take account of the context within Fanon's analysis of the potential revolutionary role that he assigns to the lumpenproletariat. Fanon described the lumpenproletariat as the spearhead of a rebellion which is led by the former illegal minority of a moderate nationalist party who have found and begun to make use of the genuine nationalism of the peasantry (Frantz Fanon, *The Wretched of the Earth*, p. 100). It is the close links of the lumpenproletariat with the peasantry and the fact that they have failed to become members of the pampered urban proletariat (ibid., p. 86) which draws them into the rebellion Fanon is describing: 'the rebellion, which began in the country districts, will filter into the towns through that fraction of the peasant population . . . which has not yet succeeded in finding a bone to gnaw in the colonial system' (ibid., p. 102). There is no evidence in 'Song of Prisoner' that such a situation of rebellion exists, although there is a lot of illustration of the continuing close contacts of the poverty-stricken prisoners with their families in the rural areas and mention of such a rebellion, if it existed, would have been inevitable. Both critics also failed to take note of the hireling status of the prisoner, another likely development within the lumpenproletariat that Fanon also noted:

> . . . if the rebellion's leaders think it will be able to develop without taking the masses into consideration the lumpenproletariat will throw itself into the battle and will take part in the conflict—but this time on the side of the oppressor.
> (ibid., p. 109)

Fanon illustrates this role of the lumpenproletariat with a reference to how 'the Congo's enemies made use of it to organize "spontaneous" mass meetings against Lumumba . . .' (loc. cit.). The landless peasants of the Acoli furnished the army of the colonialists with troops, much satirized by the '*lucak wer*' and by Okot in *Lak Tar*, for the 'white man's feud' of the 1940s and again for the colonial oppressor in Kenya during the emergency in the 1950s. In 'Song of Prisoner' their descendants have provided conflicting black agents of the neo-colonial oppressor not only with an assassin, but with a bodyguard who 'organized . . . meetings' (p. 117) that were no doubt labelled spontaneous, and with a number of prison warders who are also torturers. The poem presents us with the unedifying spectacle of members of the lumpenproletariat in the hire of one group from the bourgeoisie, or perhaps of their military successors, beating other members who have themselves had the hireling roles of bodyguard and assassin for other members of the bourgeoisie. The futility of this situation is the justification for the vagrant prisoner's despair.

The only singer who appears to have clean hands is the dismissed minister, yet he is in fact the villain of the situation. He is Ocol, or one of his friends, who had not the ears to hear the worries of Lawino for the health of the homestead or the threats of the beggar to the stability of the state, and is now himself suffering some of the ugly consequences of his actions. He confesses his responsibility:

> I am responsible
> For Law and Order
> I am responsible
> For Peace and Goodwill
> In the Land
> I am your minister
> You are my officers
> I command you . . .
> ('*Song of Prisoner*', p. 83)

He is directly responsible for the guards, his officers but now his torturers, but in claiming responsibility for 'Peace and Goodwill' he mocks himself even more by claiming the whole poisoned situation that has trapped the other singers in their mime of mutual destruction as his handiwork. If the prisoners are seen as individuals, Margaret Marshment's speculation as to the relationship of the assassin and the minister (see above, p. 79) is a little far-fetched: in so far as the voices are all representatives of different social groups, it is valid. The minister represents that social group who failed to provide any creative role for the growing lumpenproletariat that was one of the legacies of the colonial regime and encouraged its growth by their failure to put the correct resources into the countryside, then eventually turned to it for help in the gang warfare which followed when their feeble regimes began to disintegrate in the struggles for power within the bourgeoisie.

The inclusion of the 'minister' in 'Song of Prisoner', like the role of Ocol in *Song of Lawino* and *Song of Ocol*, directs our attention back on the opportunities and failures of the black élite. In a slightly different context from that suggested by Atieno Odhiambo, it does raise the question 'couldn't we have done otherwise?' ('Two Songs, a Discussion, 1', p. 108) for them, the audience to whom it is chiefly directed. Okot's poems do imply an answer to that question, which we look at in the next chapter when we examine the poems in relation to Okot's academic work and look at the ways in which the 'singers' may be seen as 'mouthpieces' rather than 'butts' of his satire.

Notes to Chapter 7

1. See Taban lo Liyong, *Eating Chiefs*, pp. 27–8; R. M. Bere, 'Land and Chieftainship among the Acoli', and D. O. Ocheng, 'Land Tenure in Acoli', *Uganda Journal*, Vol. XIX, No. 1, (March 1955), pp. 49–59.
2. This account of clans and chiefdoms follows J. K. Girling, *The Acholi of Uganda*, pp. 55–124. I have replaced his terminology ('village' and 'domain') with 'clan' and 'chiefdom' which are more commonly used in descriptions of Acoli society.
3. Conversation with Okot p'Bitek.
4. Conversation with Okot p'Bitek.
5. Conversation with Okot p'Bitek.

8 Myth Making

BECAUSE of their thematic organization and the existence of elements of dialogue within them (see above, pp. 20–4 and 62), *Song of Lawino*, *Song of Ocol*, and 'Song of Malaya' may be discussed as examples of what Northrop Frye calls 'Menippean satire': 'The short form of the Menippean satire is usually a dialogue or colloquy in which the dramatic interest is in a conflict of ideas rather than of character' (*Anatomy of Criticism*, p. 310). The 'Menippean satire' does not concentrate on the 'social behaviour' of its characters but on the ideas that lie behind that social behaviour:

> The Menippean satire deals less with people as such than with mental attitude. Pedants, bigots ... enthusiasts ... are handled in terms of their occupational approach to life as distinct from their social behaviour. The Menippean satire thus resembles the confession in its ability to handle abstract ideas and theories, and differs from the novel in its characterization which is stylized rather than naturalistic and presents people as mouthpieces of the ideas they represent.
> (ibid. p. 309)

The malaya can only be seen as the mouthpiece of a particular set of ideas as her 'social behaviour' is untrue to that of the social type she represents (see above, p. 99); both Lawino and Ocol may be seen as mouthpieces of particular ideas, despite the elements of accurate representation of their social behaviour that we have looked at. The three poems taken together are a 'colloquy' on value conflicts in contemporary Ugandan society. 'Song of Prisoner' lacks the elements of dialogue and has fictional rather than thematic organization (see above, pp. 21, 62 and 76–82), the prisoners show less interest in abstract ideas than the other singers and cannot be seen as mouthpieces of ideas. The poem nevertheless contributes to the same 'vision of the world in terms of a single intellectual pattern' (*Anatomy of Criticism*, p. 310) as the other poems.

The approach to Okot's poems developed in the last chapter places them in the context of Fanon's Marxist analysis of Africa's problems. Marxists see the cultural problem of Ocol's internalized inferiority and his confrontation with Lawino and her urban counterparts as a reflection of the working out of forces which are ultimately economic. Grant Kamenju summarizes this:

> Fanon has argued that although the system of colonization is essentially a system of economic exploitation and political oppression it is also by virtue of that very fact a process of 'inferiorization' in which racism becomes the 'intellectual unfolding' of this inferiorization.
> ('Black Aesthetics and Pan-African Emancipation', p. 178)

Thus the suppression of cultural expression of which Ocol is both the exemplar in his own life and the agent in his attempts to impose it on others is a consequence of the conditions that are created by neo-colonialism in which the black bourgeoisie are only the local agents of a capitalism controlled from outside Africa. In his Introduction to Okot's collection of essays, *Africa's Cultural Revolution*, Ngugi wa Thiong'o noted a lack of awareness of economic forces in Okot's academic work:

> While I agree with p'Bitek's call for a cultural revolution, I sometimes feel that he is in danger of emphasizing culture as if it could be divorced from its political and economic basis. (p. xii).

In this modest murmur of dissent, Ngugi considerably understates the case; Okot has specifically rejected economics as the root cause of the value conflicts he describes. In the final section of *African Religions in Western Scholarship*, entitled 'Some Conclusions', he deals summarily with Communism and Marxism. He first accepts as unalterable fact what he calls 'The rejection of Communism by most African leaders' and attributes this to the lack of a significant capitalist class within African peasant communities and to repulsion at 'the inhumanities of Communism and its totalitarian excesses'. Then he says that, after rejecting capitalism, the African leaders' 'approach to Marxism was very selective and discriminating, borrowing only what suited their interests'. After this brief excursion into economics, he turns back to the religious questions that are the subject of the book for the final word about the direction in which to look for clues to Africa's future:

> The most critical decisions which leaders of Africa must take lie not so much in the economic or political fields but in the fields of culture and basic human values. Of course there are conflicts between political philosophies and economic systems; there is also the rivalry between power blocks. But the basic conflict is between the fundamental assumptions of Western civilization and the fundamental assumptions of African civilization.
> (*African Religions in Western Scholarship*, pp. 117–19)

Okot does not ignore the economic basis of his cultural revolution; rather he denies that economic basis and contradicts Marx by asserting the primacy of religious and cultural expression over economics.

One result of Okot's lack of interest in economics and low evaluation of the strength of economic forces is the very pale reflection of economic forces in his poems. Leonard Kibera's novel *Voices in the Dark*, like Okot's poems, explores the post-Independence influence of Europe on Africa through the medium of the conflict between the urban, Westernized rich, represented by those who eat on Esitarap Road (Leonard Kibera, *Voices in the Dark*, pp. 148–60), on the one hand, and Mama Njeri (ibid., pp. 115–36), the villager like Lawino fighting Westernization and the lumpenproletariat, the beggars (pp. 15–30), like Okot's vagrant prisoner, on the other. Whereas in Okot's poems white men are figures of the past, influential now only through their imitators, in Kibera's novel they are still very much present in the persons of expatriate bosses and lecturers (p. 35), and in constant references to capitalists and the English origin of all the paraphernalia of contemporary life in Nairobi (e.g. p. 12). In Kibera's novel Wilna's father, the chief representative of the black bourgeoisie, unlike Okot's playboy-politician Ocol, is a businessman, a director of eighteen companies (p. 149), and even Mama Njeri is drawn into the town by her poverty (p. 131). Money is demonstrably the root cause of the conflicts in Kibera's novel, cutting across even the closest loyalties of the days of the fight for freedom, as Kimura explains to his fellow beggar, Irungu: 'As I always tell you, Irungu . . . never trust any B.A. neighbour on the payroll whether he fought in the forest or not. Too much to lose, too soft, all too soft' (pp. 29–30). Gerald Timundu is trapped by his inability to survive without being on the payroll of the 'Pineapple Juice Company incorporated in Birmingham, England' (p. 36), his refusal to knuckle under to the constant humiliations of working with Patrick Benson (p. 142), and his fear that marriage to Wilna will make him 'too soft' (p. 83).

The economic nexus of neo-colonialism is not evident in Okot's poems unless that one reference to Ocol as 'the dog of the white man' (p. 204; see above, p. 119) is interpreted in terms of the guarding of property. In 'Song of Malaya' and *Song of Lawino* even money is peripheral: Okot's malaya, very unlike Oculi's Rosa, does not appear to be desperately poor and the economic nature of her relationship with her clients is only once mentioned. In striking contrast to Kibera's Njoki who, in her one appearance of only a few lines in *Voices in the Dark*, extorts the required 'forty shillings' from the editor's young son (p. 14), the malaya tells us that she charged her schoolboy lover 'no fee' because he made her feel 'Ten years younger' (pp. 129–30). Despite her casual admission on one occasion that she 'has need of money' (p. 215), Lawino is very little concerned with her own poverty and repeatedly denies her desire to have a share of the expensive gifts that Ocol showers on Clementine. She only comments on the gap in wealth between Ocol and herself in Section 11 (p. 195) in the context of politics and in general and not personal terms. This same gap in wealth is much more significant in *Song of Ocol* when Ocol confronts his constituents and the beggar, but nothing in the poem suggests that Ocol's puppet masters in Europe have any control over his behaviour through economic strings: Ocol is the sole villain and the implication seems to be that, if he could only rid himself of his 'apemanship' complex (see *Africa's Cultural Revolution*, pp. 1–5), his society could shed its borrowed European clothes including not only the English labels of its dignitaries but the emerging class system as well. In contrast with Kibera, there is no indication of the need to break economic ties with Europe. The lecture he gave in Lusaka in 1967, 'Indigenous Social Ills', confirms this interpretation with its attack on the 'growing tendency in Africa for people to believe that most of our ills are imported, that the real source of our problems lies outside. We blame colonialists, imperialists, mercenaries and neo-colonialists' (*Africa's Cultural Revolution*, p. 6). Okot insists that 'most of our social ills are indigenous . . . the primary sources of our problems are native' (loc. cit.).

Atieno Odhiambo comments on the lack of objective analysis of the cause of the situation in 'Song of Prisoner'. As he identifies the prisoner as a person for Okot (see above, p. 61), he directs his criticisms against the assassin prisoner: he says that the prisoner 'does not analyse the objective reasons why it was possible for the tragedy of decadence on the part of the leaders to happen' and therefore fails to raise the question 'Couldn't we have done otherwise?' with its implications for the 'consequent question. Where do we go from here?' ('*Two Songs*, a Discussion, 1', p. 108). In the fictional world of 'Song of Prisoner' such demands cannot be answered: as Aloo Ojuka reminds Atieno Odhiambo, the assassin prisoner is a helpless man ('Two Songs, a Discussion, 2', p. 122) and this can equally well be said of all the prisoner voices. The prisoners do not understand what is happening to them; they are victims of social machinery which is out of control. The poverty of the lumpenproletariat prisoners has driven them into the town and then into the arms of the employers who have given them their futile violent occupations and the minister, a spoilt child of colonialism and the post-colonial period, has no capacity to accept his fall from a position of privilege, let alone analyse the reasons for it. It would be more consistent for Atieno Odhiambo to ask his question of the minister, as he has the know-how that Atieno Odhiambo says the bourgeoisie has denied to others in society ('Two Songs, a Discussion, 1', p. 112); but to demand it of any of these characters is to ignore the fictional mould that Okot has created for them: their inability to understand what is happening to them is an essential feature of the portrayal of the machinery of repression.

If Atieno Odhiambo's criticisms are directed against Okot instead of the prisoners, they deserve more careful consideration; it would be legitimate to criticize Okot if he had failed to answer the questions Atieno Odhiambo raises, but it means suggesting that the dramatis personae and the whole fictional content of the poem need to be changed. Atieno Odhiambo indicates what kind of analysis of the situation would have suited him:

> The task is to tell the people what capitalism implies for their lives in the future. The evils, the iniquities and the logical inability of capitalism to solve our basic problems must be so revealed that the people are left in no doubt about the fact that their bourgeois leadership is leading them to doom.
> (ibid., p. 109)

He is concerned that Okot has not represented the economic forces at work in his society and this concern is a reasonable one which could, as we have seen, be applied to all the poems. Okot's cultural revolution has an economic objective, but it is very vague:

> Can we not electrify the whole of our countryside? Must our people continue to live in unhygienic surroundings? Can we not resolve to erect better homes of permanent material for all our people? Africa must create a New Village on scientific lines.
> (*Africa's Cultural Revolution*, p. 87)

Rather than expanding on this objective, he leaves things economic and material there and turns back to the issue of fundamental assumptions:

> The crucial question arises. What kind of village? What assumptions, what social philosophy or 'world views' will guide us in the reconstruction of post-uhuru Africa?
> (loc. cit.)

This formula is not precise enough to lead to the urgent changes that Okot thinks are necessary. The cadres of Okot's 'revolution' will not move from their festivals into the work of building the 'New Village' until his economic goals and the means he will use to achieve them are more clearly defined. That having been said, it is an injustice to Okot to suggest that because he does not give a Marxist analysis of the situation behind 'Song of Prisoner' he gives no analysis at all. Okot's vision of the roots of the problems described in his poems reflects his own experience and his attitude to the function of myths within a society. In a situation where, because of their education, prospective revolutionaries share the cultural alienation from the peasantry of the bourgeois élite they wish to attack, Okot's view of his society is a very important one.

Economics has not played a major role in any of Okot's courses of study and there seem to be no parallels in his life to those experiences in England which, Mazisi Kunene notes, 'settled Ngugi's socialist conviction' (Mazisi Kunene Introduction to Ngugi wa Thiongo, *Homecoming*, p. xiii). In Chapter 1 we noted the tension between Okot's enjoyment of oral literature and the pressures against oral literature from the missionary schools (see above, p. 2). This conflict seems to have continued, not only while he was a teacher in Gulu, when it must have been intensified by the fact that one of his subjects was religious knowledge, but even while he was doing the education diploma at Bristol. He was given considerable help by some Christians among his teachers who also sought to consolidate his Christian faith, but only succeeded in forcing him to articulate his resentment of missionary suppression of African cultural expression. By his own account, his Christianity was largely nominal throughout his schooling and short teaching career, except for a period of religious enthusiasm at secondary school when, much to his mother's disgust, he was 'saved' by a visiting mission, but it was only under the challenge of his teachers at Bristol in the different atmosphere of England that his disbelief became important to him and his strong opposition to much in missionary activity was formulated.[1]

Okot's interest in African religious ideas can thus be seen as an extension of his interest in oral literature, fertilized by his nationalism and his reaction against his own missionary background. This interest either dates from, or was very much stimulated by, his research for his Oxford thesis which contains in embryo many of the major ideas expressed in his later published works, including an explanation of the link that he sees between oral literature and religious ideas:

> The texts are what generations of poets, priests, elders have composed and used. These are the small élite or intellectual class, who in any society, because of their special social position and mental and emotional equipment, lead and direct, express and interpret, the thoughts and beliefs of their communities. It is essential that we should turn to them and their works first, before we generalize about the beliefs of their people.
> ('Oral Literature Among the Acoli and Lang'o', p. 190)

Religion of the Central Luo, his study of the religion of his own people, has many sections taken from his Oxford thesis and makes extensive use of oral literature to exemplify the religious ideas he is discussing. The study of social anthropology at last gave him the opportunity to turn the weapon of 'education' that the missionaries had given him back upon them in the interests of the future Ugandan nation. His thesis begins its discussion of Acoli religious ideas with a critique of previous accounts of Acoli religion by white explorers and missionaries from Sir Samuel Baker onwards very similar to that in Chapter 3 of *Religion of the Central Luo* (ibid., pp. 179ff.; cf. *Religion of the Central Luo*, pp. 41–56), which can also be seen as a precursor of much more widely ranging criticisms of missionary approaches to all African religions in *African Religions in Western Scholarship*. While missionaries are the main whipping boys of this book, and, as Peter Rigby noted (Peter Rigby, review of *African Religions in Western Scholarship*, p. 76), Christian prejudices and theological approaches are often included even when anthropological analyses are the ostensible subject of a chapter, Okot extends his criticisms of commentators on African religions both backwards and forwards in time from the missionaries to include everyone who has written about them from the ancient Greeks to his fellow academics in East Africa. From classical times to the time of Rousseau, a number of stereotype images of the African circulated around Europe. These can be summarized as seeing the African either as a monstrous 'wild man' or as a 'noble savage' with a virtue in innocence beyond the reach of the sophisticated. None of these was based on analysis of or even interest in the realities of Africa, each being primarily 'a conceptual tool that Western scholars used in their analysis and criticisms of Western society. (*African Religions in Western Scholarship*, p. 39). Social anthropologists, seeing Africa as an area for colonial exploitation, made use of concepts like 'primitive' and 'tribe' to justify colonialism, whilst missionaries were concerned to ensure a role for Christianity in Africa and therefore, despite their increasing willingness for 'dialogue', have never been interested in them for their own sake.

His most original criticism is directed against contemporary students of African religions, mainly his fellow African scholars in the fields of anthropology or theology. They have expressed their African nationalism by proclaiming the value of African religions, discovering in them concepts that missionaries thought they had brought into Africa. This leads Okot into basic questions about the nature of Christianity itself. He says that Judaism:

> ... was very simple, involving nothing metaphysical. The 'Good News' was about the coming of a Messiah who would bring them earthly prosperity and victory over their enemies. . . .
> (*African Religions in Western Scholarship*, pp. 83–4)

He contrasts this with 'the Greek teaching ... that the sensible world, in space and time, is an illusion; and that . . . a man can live in the eternal world of "ideas" which alone is real' (loc. cit). The first Christians, he says, preached

Christianity as reformed Judaism; rather than indulging in metaphysical speculation they anticipated that 'Christ would shortly return to earth, and assisted by angelic hosts, overthrow the Roman empire and establish a theocracy in Jerusalem'. Only when it spread into the 'Graeco–Roman world' did Christianity become 'Hellenic' (loc. cit.) and adopt the metaphysical concepts which are expressed, for example, in the beginning of St John's Gospel. He attributes many of the difficulties experienced by missionaries in Africa to the absence of metaphysical speculation from traditional religions. Because of this, he sees very great danger in the metaphysical speculation about African religions which Mbiti, for example, confesses to: 'What therefore is "African Philosophy", may not amount to more than simply my own process of philosophizing the items under consideration' (John Mbiti, *African Religions and Philosophy*, pp. 1 and 2). For Okot, such 'philosophizing' leads to the creation of new African deities, not the description of existing ones:

> African peoples may describe their deities as 'strong' but not 'omnipotent'; 'wise', not 'omniscient'; 'old' not 'eternal', 'great', not 'omnipresent'. The Greek metaphysical terms are meaningless in African thinking. . . . The African deities of the books . . . are . . . creations of the students of African religions. They are all beyond recognition to the ordinary Africans in the countryside.
> (*African Religions in Western Scholarship*, p. 88)[2]

He takes the argument a step further in a blatant piece of the 'intellectual smuggling' (loc. cit.) of which he has just accused his fellow scholars when he draws support for his rejection of metaphysical thought from the decline of metaphysical theology in Europe. This section again illustrates his belief in the primacy of ideas over historical forces. Though he acknowledges the existence of 'sociological and historical explanations' for the turmoil within the Christian churches, he believes that the 'revolution in philosophy' of the rejection of metaphysics is 'at the core' of the problem (ibid., p. 91).

The preoccupation of all these groups with something other than African religions has meant that all their works 'leave the proper study of African religions untouched' (ibid., p. 107). To avoid the errors that arise from the imposition of alien superstructures on African religious practices, it is vital that present studies 'describe' rather than 'interpret' these practices:

> What is required now is a number of descriptive works from different areas of Africa, which will enable us to carry out comparative analysis in African religions. It is from this exercise that we shall be able to generalize about African religions and philosophy.
> (*Africa's Cultural Revolution*, p. 93)

Okot's study *Religion of the Central Luo* contains a historical introduction dealing with certain controversies in relation to the history of Luo communities in Uganda, a refutation of a number of metaphysical theories as to the nature of *jok*, and a description of the ritual activities that are directed towards various *jogi* (plural of *jok*). He deliberately avoids any definition of the nature of *jok* because 'the Nilotes are concerned not with ontological definitions but with dynamic function' (*African Religions in Western Scholarship*, pp. 72–3) and therefore the only interpretation he ever gives of ritual activities, usually drawn out of him by the need to refute other interpretations, explains the activities in terms of their social functions. Of ancestor worship, for example, he says:

> Its significance as a way of interpreting ill-health and misfortune was only nominal. . . . More important is the way in which the belief operated to unify lineage groups and to strengthen the bonds of relationship between members of the group.
> (*Religion of the Central Luo*, p. 104)

Okot looks at all beliefs in terms of their 'dynamic function'. In an unpublished paper 'Myths and Nation Building', presented to the Staff Seminar of the History Department at Nairobi University in February 1972, he first considers Greek mythology briefly and notices how people in Western Europe have created a mythology around the Greeks which is of value to them because it links them to Greek civilization and therefore 'preaches the superiority of the white man over all other peoples'. He justifies his functional view of mythology by reference to other social anthropologists and summarizes the function of myths: 'in general myths are reckoned to embody a system of beliefs common to the society and to express and support a set of basic social ideas and values'. He incorporates into the realm of mythology, so defined, all literature and all the social sciences, explicitly rejecting the claim of Marxists to a uniquely 'scientific' view of society and emphasizing that all myths are fictitious: 'The critical point is this, that mythologies are not dependent on success because they are true. They move men not because they can be proved scientifically . . .' (ibid.). This idea that the fictitious nature of a mythology is unrelated to its success in performing its social functions explains why Okot has put so much effort into the understanding of African religions even though he himself is not a believer in them: 'I am neither a Christian nor a pagan. I do not believe in witchcraft or supernatural forces' (Okot p'Bitek, 'Reflect, Reject, Recreate', *East Africa Journal*, p. 31).

He has also expressed doubt as to whether African deities will 'survive the revolutions in science and philosophy which have killed the Christian God' (*African Religions in Western Scholarship*, p. 112); as the chiefdom deities of the Acoli have perished in the changing political circumstances of recent years, so may the remaining practices which continue to help people deal with disease and to bind the members of a clan together. However, he is convinced that, at the present time, 'apart from a handful of us [non-believers], all our people have a full-blooded religious system'. (loc. cit.) For the majority of Africans, those beliefs are still performing their social functions.

In this situation of flux, that 'handful of non-believers', who are the 'educated' élite whom Ocol represents in Okot's fictional world, have the opportunity and the duty to create the new mythology which will be the foundation of the desirable future African society. Despite their experience of cultural exile they are the only possible heirs to those 'generations of poets, priests, elders' whose wisdom expressed through oral literature directed and interpreted the 'thoughts and beliefs of their communities' (see above, p. 132). This responsibility devolves particularly on the 'scholar seeking after truth', whom Ocol pictures sweating amidst his 'mountains of books' (p. 83):

> ... It is critically important to bear in mind that myth-making and myth-propagating are the central functions of social anthropology and the other related subjects such as history, sociology, political science, religious studies, philosophy and literature.
> ('Reflect, Reject, Recreate', p. 29)

There are two challenges before these African scholars, first 'to destroy all the myths that were used by the colonialists to dominate us' and secondly 'to create new and Afro-centred myths on which to reconstruct our new nations in our own interests (loc. cit.)'. These are the tasks Okot's singers are fulfilling when they act as mouthpieces of conflicting ideas.

In *Song of Lawino*, Ocol supports the missionary teachers in their propagation of the Christian myth of creation. Because of the functional nature of Acoli religion, speculation about the origin and nature of the universe was new to Lawino when the missionaries introduced their tales of a creator God. When she becomes entangled in such speculation she attacks her teachers partly for their refusal to answer questions; Lawino wishes she could find someone to help her who would not get angry so easily. Their failure to answer questions makes them bad pastors on their own terms:

> A young tree that is bending
> They do not like to straighten. (p. 147)

When she suggests that perhaps they 'Have no answers' (p. 148) she is also attacking the futility of the whole exercise of metaphysical speculation which creates explanations of existence containing irreconcilable contradictions. Ocol also propagates the myth that all African medicine and ritual is worthless as a way of dealing with problems in the community and that European medicine can replace it completely. Despite his belief in angels (p. 153), Ocol considers the whole of the Acoli spirit world to be a set of 'foolish superstitions' and their 'herbalists' to be 'liars' who only ever succeed 'by accident' as their preparations are so unhygienic (pp. 153–8). Lawino responds with an appeal for a more balanced and tolerant view: both European and Acoli medicines have their strengths and weaknesses. In defence of this assertion, she presents a very full account of the Acoli way of dealing with disease and misfortune. As Okot does in *Religion of the Central Luo*, she treats ritual activities as an extension of medicine:

> The beliefs and practices I have described and certain knowledge of medicines were used to diagnose, explain, interpret the individual cause of misfortune and ill-health, and they also provided means and ways of coping with individual situations of anxiety and stress.
> (*Religion of the Central Luo*, p. 160)

In Section 10, Lawino refers to all the types of *jok* Okot mentions in his study except chiefdom *jok* which has been in decline with the decline of the traditional chiefdom.[3]

The most serious calamities are beyond the reach of either Acoli or white man's medicine because they are misfortunes that 'have a root' (p. 165) in some failure of observance or some abuse within the clan community. The curse of 'your uncle' (that is *nero*, mother's brother) is directed only against children, and reminds them of their relationship with their mother's clansmen because of their fear of uncontrollable bed-wetting (ibid., pp. 148–9). The curses of parents are very rare because they destroy the family through the insanity and impotence they bring to the son: 'when he cursed his son the father was also causing the worst harm to himself because it was through his son that he lived on; so that to curse the son the father was also killing himself' (ibid., pp. 150–1). The existence of these curses which are so rarely used strengthens the sense of responsibility in both parents and children. When calamities of various types trouble a whole clan equally, the abuse must have been done to the dead members of the clan, the ancestors, who have been neglected in the clan shrine and the whole clan community must gather to feed the ancestors and pray to the dead, for their troubles to be taken away by the setting sun (p. 170). In *Religion of the Central Luo* Okot suggests that the Acoli see clear limits to the power of their rituals to protect them from disaster. He interprets the words '*Woko*', '*Wi-lobo*', and '*Ru-piny*', which some scholars have linked to belief in 'a high god', in terms of a sceptical fatalism in the face of the most serious problems of existence which cannot be averted by medical or ritual means: '*Wi-lobo* and *Woko* represents the problems, risks, sufferings that the individual faced during his lifetime. *Ru-piny* represented those of each day' (ibid., pp. 154–6). Lawino's words about 'Mother Death', illustrate Okot's final words in *Religion of the Central Luo*:

> . . . when all these failed, when the game of ritually acting out their deeply felt needs, desires and hopes had produced no satisfactory results . . . the Central Luo became sceptical and irreligious, and preferred to face the facts of life coolly and realistically. When your son died you wept, but amid tears, you declared '*Wi-lobo*': 'This is the way of the world.'
> (ibid., p. 160)

Lawino tells us that 'No one can stop you . . . when the day has dawned / For the journey to Pagak' (p. 172).

The malaya attempts to destroy the Christian mythology surrounding sexual behaviour and to propagate or create the myth that traditional African societies placed very few restrictions on the enjoyment of sexual pleasure. In his concluding chapter in *African Religions in Western Scholarship*, Okot picks out 'the concept of family' as 'one of the basic issues of nation building'. Having mentioned the legal tangles that resulted from the imposition of colonial marriage laws on traditional practice, he says that 'the root of the problem . . . is the African idea of sex and marriage' (pp. 113–14). He discusses the effect of St Paul's 'sex hatred' on Christian sexual ethics and contrasts these with the attitude of the Acoli:

> The word fornication means voluntary sexual intercourse between two unmarried persons, or two persons not married to each other. In most African societies, having sexual intercourse with married women by persons other than their husbands is strictly forbidden; but unmarried women enjoy both married and unmarried men. In northern Uganda mothers encourage their daughters to sleep with their boyfriends and test their manhood before marriage. (p. 11)

This contrast presents African leaders with a problem which Okot considers to be of very great importance:

> It is important for African leaders to consider whether sexual ethics in their countries should be based on St Paul's prejudice against women and sex, or built on the African viewpoint which takes sex as a good thing. (p. 11)

In his review of *Two Songs*, R. C. Ntiru sees the main thrust of 'Song of Malaya' as an attack on hypocrisy:

> ... p'Bitek's point, as I take it, is that for as long as the policeman sleeps with the prostitute tonight and arrests her tomorrow, for as long as the MP passes the slum clearance law and hires the prostitute a suburban bungalow, for as long as the Supreme Planning Commission retires to arrange favours of prostitutes after serious deliberations on social development, inevitably for so long shall prostitution remain with us. . . .
> (R. C. Ntiru, review of *Two Songs*, in *East Africa Journal*, p. 39–40)

Hypocrisy is only occasionally the subject of the malaya's attack. She is not chiefly concerned to isolate and attack these individuals who fail to practise what they preach; she is attempting to illustrate that no one practises that morality because it places unnatural restrictions on 'good' sexual desires.

The malaya celebrates the universality of sexual desire and attacks impediments to its fulfilment. The first section establishes the festival mood with its cumulative descriptions of pent-up sexual desire at last free to look for satisfaction. Many of those she welcomes into her house are from outside the city and have months or years of frustration behind them. She begins with the most frustrated, the sailor, soldier, and newly released prisoner, then there are miners and engineers on rural projects, teachers from 'bush schools', businessmen attending conferences, and 'bus drivers' and 'taxi men' who have to stay away from home overnight. These 'hungry lions' compete with the 'factory workers' and 'shop assistants' and the 'leader of the People' himself as they hunt the malayas (pp. 127–32). The mood returns when the 'Angel Prostitutes' are asked to 'Bear these wretches / Into your heaven!' (p. 154). Sexual desire and its fulfilment are as inevitable as the succession of day and night:

> Who can command
> The sun
> Not to rise in the morning?
> Or having risen
> Can hold it
> At noon
> And stop it
> From going down
> In the west? (p. 184)

The hypocrites are mistaken in their beliefs, not in their actions; when they succumb to sexual desire they show their health and normality and participate in the festival that the malaya is presiding over.

The first impediment to sexual fulfilment that the malaya deals with is the 'one pest' remaining in Africa, venereal disease. She appeals to all those with influence, from headmasters to presidents, to divert all their resources and their revolutionary energy to its eradication. The major impediment, however, is the imported Christian morality of monogamy which is the source of the enmity of all those who attack her. The most voluble and bitter of her enemies are those Westernized wives who have been led to expect to retain sole possession of their husbands and are therefore violently jealous and angry about their interest in other women. The malaya asks where the wives learnt their attitudes: did their mothers not teach them their duty to please their husbands, did their fathers not teach them to accept that their husbands would have other women (pp. 149–50)? The malaya provides the answer when she mocks the black bishop, the illegitimate son of a polygamist, caricaturing his morality with the question:

> Do you actually pray
> To God
> To bless each bee
> So that it should
> Stick to one flower? (p. 162)

'Song of Malaya' hints at the question which is discussed in *African Religions in Western Scholarship* as to where the bishop himself got his morality. St Paul's uncompromising disapproval of sexual desire 'if they cannot contain let them marry, for it is better to marry than to burn' is contrasted with 'Christ's more humane attitude to women' as displayed by his tolerance of the prostitute who anointed his feet and his response to the accusers of the woman taken in adultery: 'He that is without sin among you, let him first cast a stone at her' (*African Religions in Western Scholarship*, p. 116). The malaya asks the 'bush teacher'

> How dare you
> Throw the first stone
> While Christ writes
> In the sand? (p. 173)

As well as attacking hypocrisy, this question challenges the very basis of the mythology of the malaya's accusers.

The malaya is an inadequate spokesman of African ideas of sexual behaviour because of her isolation; she is not part of a family. Okot only hints at this as a limitation in her way of life when she confesses to being 'Deadly lonely' and admits that her son is miserable and might be missing a father (pp. 170–1). As her references to her parents and brothers show, the malaya is as isolated from her former family as the black bishop must be from his and she is part of no new family. Okot cannot afford to elaborate on this and show its real consequences without destroying the mood of celebration he has chosen to express in the poem. Okot's assertion of the African attitude to sexual pleasure arises out of a discussion of the role of the family; he explains a mother's encouragement of her daughter's pre-marital sexual activities in terms of the need to be sure a potential husband is fertile and quotes with approval from Taylor's *Primal Vision* 'the wonder of sex maturing lies in the fact that by its means a boy or girl literally attains Manhood and becomes a link in the living chain of humanity' (ibid., p. 117). Bishop Keith Russell explains the conflicts over sexual behaviour that arose in the newly formed Anglican church in terms of the insensitivity on the part of the missionaries to the values associated with polygamous family life. The importance of fertility in the concept of manhood, womanhood, and marriage is shown by the fact that the Acoli young man sleeps with his bride when only the first part of the marriage negotiations have been completed and the final instalment of the bride wealth will only be paid if she becomes pregnant and then after the birth of the baby. This emphasis on fertility provides a strong inducement to pre-marital sex, since if you have already borne someone else's child you cannot be the partner to blame if a marriage is childless. In addition to its opposition to this pre-marital sexual activity, the church insistently opposed polygamy. Early readers in the *ot kwan* were perfectly willing to bless their first marriage with a church service whilst completing bride wealth negotiations in the normal way, but they expected to be able to take a second wife, especially if the first marriage produced no surviving children. Their exclusion from church services following the marriage of a second wife when the first one proved barren was initially incomprehensible to the converts since it prevented them from fulfilling a basic need in their lives, producing children to prove their fertility, look after them in old age, and ensure their continued influence after death through activities at the ancestral shrine (J. K. Russell, *Men Without God?*, pp. 49–53).

Once or twice the malaya shows respect for the association of sexual activities with having children and even looking after them properly. She contemptuously contrasts the behaviour of the bishop who did not make love to a woman with that of her grandfather who had ten wives and looked after all their children (p, 163). She appears to have no fear herself of having children, her 'three sons' by one man easily cap the 'two daughters' his wife has given him (p. 150) and she later contrasts her fertility with the wives who eat 'lizard eggs' contraceptive pills (p. 151). Her attitude in this section is not reconciled with the admission of the unhappiness of her fatherless son and despite these few references to the value of children, the poem largely separates, as prostitution must, the 'good' pleasure of sex from the idea of the 'link in the living chain of humanity'. Her fertility may provide proof of manhood to some men but the 'Gum boots' and 'boxing gloves' (pp. 141–

2) which provide necessary protection against venereal disease also inhibit conception. The idea of manhood is effectively reduced to the ability to perform sexually which provides the explosive mixture, the 'time bomb / Pulsating in your loin' (p. 127) and isolates the diseased, 'the disappointed men' with 'Their spears vomiting butter' (p. 182). The complex of ideas associated with the spear in oral literature and *Song of Lawino* (see above pp. 50–5) is now reduced to nothing more than a diseased penis.

Sexual performance is a necessary part of the symbolism of the spear and of the conception of manly behaviour in oral literature. This woman's complaint song taunts a husband for his inability to achieve what he desires:

Jalli omato kongo omer
Me layel mon;
Laco okako kongo oyeng
Dong bwolo mon,

He is drunk
And wants to trouble women for nothing;
The man is totally drunk,
He is deceiving women, he can't do it;
(*Horn of My Love*, p. 64)

The effects of venereal disease are also within the range of experience of oral literature. In the 1940s, a major victim of the *lucak wer* all over Acoliland was the soldier who fought in the Second World War and then periodically returned on leave, attracting women away from his homebound rivals by his swagger and boastful tales. One of the many taunts used against these soldiers concerned the diseases they spread amongst their women:

Twon nyac ma lakeya
Orado kom lakeya;
Lakeya kok, oyoyo,
Kok benebene . . .

The bull gonorrhoea
That the soldier smeared in the body
of my aunt's daughter;
My aunt's daughter cries, oh, oh, oh
She cries all night long . . .

However, fertility is also an essential part of manliness. Even healthy soldiers who are faithful enough to marry girls and eventually come back to them cannot fulfil a husband's duties and give their wives children because they are so long away:

Mon keya lulur,
Kerekerekere ki waraga,
Warega doko latin ce?
Mon keya lulur.

Soldiers' wives are barren;
They are always writing letters,
Can letters become children?
Soldiers' wives are barren.
(*Horn of My Love*, p. 66)

Whatever other accomplishments you have and however beautiful your wife may be, unless you have children you are a subject of mockery. The next song is directed against a victim of a phantom pregnancy. With the pressure on a young bride-to-be to have a child so that the marriage arrangements would be completed, it is not surprising that cases of this desire leading to a girl producing all the symptoms of pregnancy without the foetus have been known. The disappearance of this pregnancy was interpreted in terms of *jok ngu* (*ngu* means man-eating beasts of prey, including leopards) who had sucked up the foetus from the woman's insides:

Omera ibedo ki nyero li-kiny-kiny-kiny
Dako kono peke
Omera ma yengo gica
Omera ma jwato aula rii
Dako pari peke
Jal kelo dako ma kwac omato iye
Nywal ku kwak liwota
Omera ikelo dul okeco
Omera ma kelo beco paco
Dako to peke
Cam ber, yam ber wa con

My brother you are shaking with laughter
[seem quite happy]
[But] you have no wife
My brother shakes his *gica headgear*
My brother swings his giraffe-tail arm-swish
You have no wife
The man has brought home a woman whose inside has

been sucked by a leopard
She can never produce, my friend
My brother you have brought a log of *okeco* wood
[very hard wood, it ruined the blade of the traditional axe]
My brother has brought a beautiful one home
But there is no wife
Eat beauty, she has remained beautiful so long
(*Religion of the Central Luo*, pp. 112–13)

In the reference to the log of *okeco* wood, sexual entry itself is associated with fertility, since there is no suggestion of inadequate sexual performance, yet her failure to have children is interpreted in terms of her husband's inability to 'penetrate' her (ibid., footnote on p. 120).

In the song 'Rii rii ye' (I hear a bicycle bell; see above, p. 93) the wrong choice made by the young man was not the choice of a woman who was barren but his preference for a machine over a wife. The 'barrenness' of the machine is the basis of the *lucak wer*'s mockery and is again expressed in an image of the difficulties of sexual entry: the song ends:

Lim kor lamera,
Inyomo ki gari ba,
Iomo lela mwa,
Tun lela lal,
Rombo cundi bongo.

The bride wealth of my sister,
You use it for marrying a bicycle,
You have brought a bicycle home for nothing;
The bicycle's vagina
Is too small for your penis.
(*Horn of My Love*, p. 78)

The next song attacks a soldier, not for failing to give his wife children, but for failing to look after her. It is in the form of a dialogue between a soldier on the point of leaving to fight and a young man who is going to stay at home:

Awobe tua we
Kitino, gwoku mon gang,
Wan wacito ka celo Hitila.
    Monyi mony pa woru ce?
Otara do,
Mony dwong ya.
    Wupeny Mussolini

Youths of our homeland, listen
Children, look after our women in the homestead,
We are off to shoot [fight] Hitler.
    This battle is it your father's feud?
It is the white man's [battle],
The battle is great, oh.
    You ask Mussolini [to come and look
    after your wives and property]
('Oral Literature Among the Acoli and Lang'o', p. 310)

The boastful soldier is sure of support in his excited desire to go and 'shoot Hitler', so much so that he misses the challenge in the question 'is it your father's feud?' and takes it as a further opportunity to illustrate his warrior valour as, being the 'white man's battle', it must be very 'great'. He has therefore left himself defenceless before the suggestion that, since he has adopted the white men as his clansmen, a white man should look after his property. Whatever importance hunting and fighting prowess, or sexual performance, had in the Acoli concept of manhood, the fulfilment of the duty of having children and looking after your family was an essential part of it.

Lawino emphasizes the conflict between the myths and habits of the white man and Acoli sexual and marriage practices in many ways. Her incomprehension of the Virgin Birth is expressed in terms of Acoli marriage customs. Mary was legally married, 'The bride wealth had already been paid', yet it is said she 'did not know a man'; this is impossible since a girl visits her future husband 'To try his manhood' and the bride wealth only changes hands if 'She gets a stomach' (p. 147). The missionaries prevent these normal premarital trials with their boarding schools where the sexes are separated at the very time of life when a child should be discovering his sexual power, yet they themselves cannot contain their healthy desires: the teacher of the Evening Speakers' Class trails Lawino to the dance, and even the fattest priest

Feels better
When he touches
A girl's breasts (pp. 122–6)

In the description of the ballroom dance, Lawino picks out the possible, but uncommon, event of white people dancing with their close relatives because of the disrespect that this implies to the Acoli (p. 37). She attacks the myth of nationalism which hides the struggle of the élite for privileges from the point of view of the ideal of clan unity which political activities disrupt.

His 'education' is of course the source of Ocol's alien mythologies and is itself surrounded by the most powerful new myth. Education was always seen as a means of obtaining a new kind of power outside the realm of the clan. Rwot Ibrahim Awic's invitation to the missionaries (see above, p. 106) was a response to the external threats to his traditional power. He had already shown his adaptability in using the guns and the military organization of the Egyptians in defence of his own people before his capture by the British invaders. In Kampala, he saw a more complex administration and many new machines and also discovered that certain groups of white men were giving away their wisdom freely. The messengers he sent to Bunyoro 'said to the white people that they should come and teach his people wisdom because *their way of doing things was good*'. When the missionaries arrived the people were fascinated by the bicycle, 'the donkey that runs without any eyes' and the pills ('lizard's eggs') that they were given (K. J. Russell, *Men Without God*?, pp. 20–1, author's italics). From the beginning the Acoli associated schooling with the mastery of foreign techniques which would give a new kind of potency to the clan through a few of its members, whilst the missionaries were primarily concerned to spread Christ's gospel and only peripherally interested in passing on the white man's techniques.

In many places the initial siting of church and school in one building under the control of one catechist and teacher, who was himself the product of a very short training in a major mission centre, continued for many years. The first non-mission educational institutions were teacher training centres established in 1948 (ibid., p. 36) and missionaries have continued to have a role in former mission schools even since the independent government took control of them. Neither pupils nor teachers in the local elementary schools were able to resolve the conflict of aims between the missionaries who had trained the teachers and the clan elders who had invited the teachers into the community. Lawino caricatures the result in her description of the Evening Speakers' Class. The Acoli teacher 'spoke the same language / As the white priests' (p. 117) and tried to pass on by rote the formulae he had recently learnt:

> He shouted angrily
> As if he uttered abuses,
> We repeated the same words
> Shouting back at him
> As when you shout
> Insults at somebody's mother!
> We repeated the meaningless phrases
> Like the yellow birds
> In the *lajanawara* grass (p. 117)

Unlike the padres who confine themselves to stabbing girls' breasts with their glances and accidentally brushing them when they can, the teacher cannot keep away from the 'pagan' dances that both the padre and he himself condemn. Lawino's contempt for his clumsy attempt to seduce her throws him back into his isolation from the community who invited him to serve them and forces him to hide even more behind the mastery of the 'meaningless phrases' that the missionaries have armed him with.

Though Ocol tells us he read 'Econ.' at Makerere (*Song of Ocol*, p. 55) there is little evidence from his attitudes in either *Song* that his later education equipped him any better than that kind of elementary education for the management of the administration left by the white man. Ocol is concerned with the life style and values of his community, not with the economic techniques used to manage it. The various myths of Ocol in *Song of Lawino* are replaced in *Song of Ocol* with an extravagant faith in progress through technological change which must transform all the traditional customs of East Africa. Ocol taunts traditional Africa, not with sexual impotence, but with technological impotence and defeat at the hands of those with a stronger technology. The images of Section 1 condemn Lawino for her isolation and failure like an old wooden arrow meeting the clean modern concrete of a wall (p. 10). The gains of the Kalenjin were only a vast area of semi-desert which 'Remained 'closed' to progress' (p. 48) and even Chaka was utterly defeated; Ocol concludes:

> What proud poem
> Can we write
> For the vanquished? (p. 86)

His treatment of the spear as a poor weapon rather than a symbol shows similar insistence on the importance of technological potency over traditional manly qualities.

In the new technological world Ocol dreams of creating, the initiates are those who spent their time sweating and cramming through their schools and colleges whilst their age-mates who tested their courage by going on lone hunting expeditions are condemned as:

> Thoughtless and carefree
> Like children dancing around the hut
> After a meal; (pp. 55–6)

The only way the initiates can drag their age-mates into the new way of life is by their forcible re-education through the brutal experience of the destruction of all supports of the old way of life. The village must assemble for a final celebration in full traditional regalia of the passing of 'The Old Homestead' and then set out as 'Pilgrims to the New City' (pp. 75–80). Ocol can see no alternative to this abrupt transformation because of his belief in the inexorable spread of 'the fierce fires / Of progress and civilization' (p. 77). Rather than managing the techniques of the white man in the interest of the clan as Rwot Ibrahim Awic dreamed they would, Ocol's generation bowed down and worshipped those techniques and waited for them to destroy the clan.

With nothing but the myth of 'progress' to show for his education, Ocol is as helpless as the teacher of the Evening Speakers' Class before the disappointment and incomprehension of his community and can only hide behind the mystique that surrounds his university education. Lawino wishes to meet:

> Someone who has genuinely
> Read deeply and widely
> And not someone like my husband
> Whose preoccupation
> Is to boast in the market place
> Showing off to people! (p. 146)

When challenged about the creation myth, Ocol hides in the mystery of his great learning: Lawino's questions must be 'silly' because she has not been to school. Even if he spoke in Acoli she would not understand him, but he cannot express the complicated thoughts of a university man in a 'primitive' language like Acoli. The inevitable conclusion is that someone from a university 'Can only have useful talk' with others with the same training (pp. 140–1). This attitude forces Ocol into his loneliness and silence at home, the façade of busy-ness and obsessive punctuality maintaining the mystery surrounding his work, the dignity of his status preventing him from participating in any of the activities of the clan. The worst aspect of this attitude for Lawino is his treatment of children:

> If a child cries
> Or has a cough
> Ocol storms like a buffalo,
> He throws things
> At the child; (pp. 92–3)

Only a 'witch', a person who is compelled by some insanity to destroy people of his own clan under cover of darkness, could express so perverted an attitude, so near to a curse which would destroy him as well as his children. All the inconvenience that children bring into a home should be seen as a blessing because at the heart of the prayer at the ancestral shrine is the prayer for childbirth, since children ensure the clan's continuing survival. Whatever new powers and duties his education has brought him, he cannot escape from his responsibility to his own children.

Lawino contrasts the education the missionaries gave with the songs of the moonlight *orak* dance. She and her friends ran away from the Evening Speakers' Class,

> . . . crossed the stream
> And climbed the gentle rise
> Straight into the arena.
> We joined the line of friends
> And danced among our age-mates
> And sang songs we understood,
> Relevant and meaningful songs,
> Songs about ourselves: (p. 122)

Through these songs they learnt about their own community, its local personalities, and the values that lay behind the satire of the *orak* songs. Through the *otole* and *bwola* songs and the myths they learnt a little about their history and the nature and justification of political authority within the clan. Nearly all this Ocol and his friends missed when they were locked in their boarding schools sweating and cramming away from the evil temptations of pagan dances, yet, when they came to attempt to fulfil Rwot Awic's dream of turning the white man's learning against him and restoring political power to the Acoli, they became leaders of these communities whose mythologies they did not know. It is no wonder that they remained dependent on white man's myths. Lawino inverts the myth of potency through schooling which has had a hold on the Acoli since Lloyd's party arrived in 1906. Because reading makes a young man into a 'stump' in 'the ways of his people' the cream of Acoli young men 'Were finished in the forest' of books:

> Their manhood was finished
> In the class-rooms,
> Their testicles
> Were smashed
> With large books! (p. 208)

In relation to 'Song of Prisoner', Atieno Odhiambo asserted that the prisoners 'did not analyse the objective reasons why it was possible for the tragedy of decadence on the part of the leaders to happen' (see above, p. 130). In *Song of Lawino*, through his mouthpiece Lawino, Okot gives his analysis, but it is not expressed in economic terms. Okot believes that real power to break the economic and cultural stranglehold of Europe on Africa rested in the hands of the élite who took control at Independence and that they were incapable of using that power not because of the economic laws of history but because of their own acceptance of Europe's myths which isolated them from the communities they were supposed to lead. In 1966, when the bourgeoisie still held power in most parts of Africa, Okot believed that they could redeem themselves and still fulfil the dream of Rwot Awic as creative leaders of their people.

The responsibility for leading them to do so still devolved on the African scholars pictured in the last section of *Song of Ocol*. What they should not do, which Okot suggests through Ocol's mockery Marxists have tried to do, is build the new mythology with imported bricks:

> Tell me
> You student of communism,
> And you Professor of History
> Did Senegalese blood
> Flow in the veins
> Of Karl Marx?
> And Lenin,
> Was he born
> At Arusha? (pp. 83–4)

If, as Okot believes, the 'basic conflict' that Africans are engaged in is not between economic forces but between 'fundamental assumptions of Western civilization and the fundamental assumptions of African civilization' (see above, p. 128), such importation of ideas is merely submission to alien mythology. On this basis Okot asserts the importance of the study of African religions not only to enable the leaders of Africa to know their people better so that they may more easily transform the people's way of life, but, more important, to discover from the people the direction the projected transformation should take:

> . . . if the leaders of Africa sincerely believe that the social reconstruction of Africa should be based on the African world-view, their religions must be studied and presented as accurately as possible so as to discover the African world-view.
> (*African Religions in Western Scholarship*, p. 113)

It is in this assertion that Okot parts company from Fanon and his followers, from Nyerere, from Senghor, and from most other contemporary African thinkers.

Whilst both Okot p'Bitek and Frantz Fanon direct the eyes of African nationalist leaders to the peasantry, there is a radical difference in their attitudes in doing so. For Fanon, the great virtue of the peasantry is the fact that they have suffered most and gained least under colonialism and are therefore the group that is most determined to bring about its violent overthrow:

> . . . the mass of the country people have never ceased to think of the problem of their liberation except in terms of violence, in terms of taking back the land from the foreigners, in terms of national struggle and of armed insurrection.
> (Frantz Fanon, *The Wretched of the Earth*, p. 101)

When the alliance of nationalist leaders and peasants has been formed, the preparation for rebellion will involve some political education of the peasants by the nationalists: 'The men coming from the towns learn their lessons in the hard school of the people; and at the same time these men open classes for the people in military and political education' (loc. cit.). This education is unlikely to be enough, since Fanon says that the initial rebellion will be crushed by the determined counterattack of the enemy and the next step must involve the giving up of many of the peasants' cherished ideas, for example, his attachment to his own land rather than that of the whole nation through a further, more thorough period of education by the nationalist leaders: '. . . the leaders of the rising realize that the various groups must be enlightened; that they must be educated and indoctrinated . . .' (ibid., p. 108).[4] Okot, on the other hand, suggests, as we have seen, that such indoctrination including, as it certainly would, ideas imported into Africa, would itself mean the selling out of the cultural revolution. The leaders must in fact submit to the peasants for their own re-education in the African view of man so that the new mythologies and the political ideas that they produce will be African in origin and therefore able to perform their function as a basis for a genuinely African society.

He is attempting to be a root and branch man in his approach to Western scholarship as we have seen he is in relation to Western literary forms. He does not seek, as Senghor sought, to wed together elements of Western and African philosophy; rather, despite his occasional inconsistency in latching on to trends in Western thought which appear to suit his purpose, he seeks to eradicate the influences of Western philosophy from Africa, retaining only Western technology. He insists that the leaders of Africa must approach their people in total humility, without a hint of any of the notions they might have picked up during their student exile in Europe, and casually condemns Nyerere as a borrower of Western ideas:

> Attempts that have been made to reconstruct our new nations on the foundations of Western political ideas do not strike me as having been particularly successful. Nyerere, for example, has attempted to Africanize the concepts of socialism and democracy.
> (*Africa's Cultural Revolution*, pp. 87–9)

African leaders must turn to 'the real masters' of truly African ideas, the people in the countryside:

> What is man? What is the purpose of life in this world? How should society be ordered? We must find the answers to these fundamental questions . . . as seen by the man in the countryside.

Medicine, architecture, political science, and all the subjects in a university must be transformed by their reconstruction around African concepts of the nature of man (loc. cit.).

As a 'real master', Lawino seeks to begin the re-education of Ocol. First she must remove all the obstructions to learning that the missionaries have left with him, the 'gum', 'dust', and 'chaff' that make him deaf and the 'dark glasses' and 'scales' that blind him (p. 211). Then she sends him to the elders of the clan in whom the power of the 'living chain of humanity' resides, so that they can restore to him the 'spear' of his manhood. The spear that Ocol should trust represents not simply sexual potency but the myths of his own clan that will restore to him his independence from the white man and give him the power to be an effective leader of his own people. Through the living elders, Ocol must seek the blessing of clansmen now dead through a prayer at the ancestral shrine, that

> . . . the setting sun
> May take away all your shyness
> Deceit, childish pride and sharp tongue! (p. 213)

With their blessing, he will be able to seek the forgiveness of his mother and be ready then to fulfil his role of father and head of the family, an acceptable husband for Lawino. Okot's vision of the final chance of the sixties élite lay, not in their rapid re-education of the peasantry, but in the rapid re-education of them by the peasantry, leading to a reconciliation of old and new forms of authority and a more gradual transformation of technology in Africa, guaranteeing the continuation of many of the traditions of clan relationship.

The years between 1966 and 1971 when 'Song of Prisoner' was published were unhappy for most national groups of the bourgeoisie and brought the Ugandan élite to the brink of disaster. Lawino's vision of the rapid reconciliation of leaders and peasants was overtaken by these events. In 'Song of Prisoner' all human family contacts have been poisoned by poverty or violence and visions of peaceful family life are confined to memories, dreams, and some of the little portraits of insect or animal life. The violence not only injures the prisoners and destroys their family peace, it takes over their beings so that they themselves are destroyers; this is also reflected in images of violence and destruction from the animal and insect world. Because the poem contains no mouthpiece of Okot's ideas, it reflects them less precisely than *Song of Lawino* or 'Song of Malaya'. Nevertheless, the fiction of the poem reinforces the myth of the strength and significance of family life to manly identity for Africans and makes it into a law of nature by the animal references. In constant tension with this is autonomous violence, generated apparently by something within Africa and again reinforced by the violence of animal life.

The vagrant who is the main interpreter of life for the reader of the poem sees the world in such a lurid light that even a sunset observed from his cell is an image of bloodshed, the colours on the lake being the blood of dying animals and humans (p. 35). This prisoner also has a capacity to observe and respect gentleness, especially in a family context: the very quiet song of the ladybird 'Breaks through the high ceiling' and the vagrant visualizes her collecting nectar and carrying it back to the nest (p. 49). He sees no threat to the family life of the ladybird, but most of his visions of animal families show them to be threatened by destruction. A python eats the family of an edible rat hiding in a dead termite mound, whilst an ostrich races back to her eggs to cower over them throughout a rainstorm (p. 59). Under the shock of the assassin's shot crickets mourn, toads yell, and 'Mama frogs' make their children hide their heads from the undefined threat in the atmosphere (pp. 66–7).

Within himself he contains both the gentleness of the ladybird and the violence of the hyena. Like the 'proud cattle egret' his identity would be best expressed in front of his wife and children amongst his own clansmen, where his physical strength and his skill as a dancer and a drummer could find a peaceful outlet and he could remain in a proper relationship with his dead father. Even before his imprisonment, the poverty that had driven him into the town had robbed him of these possibilities, and now the dream of the farm-house on the hill where the children can play in the peaceful stream follows after the images of python and ostrich, of children eaten and eggs threatened by a storm. The vagrant has been employed as a bodyguard in a politician's entourage, a violent enough occupation, and his bitterness now makes him threaten desecration on the grave of his father. Part of the purpose of the two sections where he attacks his parents is to satirize what Ntiru called the 'royalistic tendency ... of African political leaders to create Royal [Presidential] Houses and Clans' (review of *Two Songs*, pp. 39–40) but the violence is out of proportion to this satirical purpose. These are further examples of the destruction of the ties of family that the society has induced.

The minister is both a victim of political violence and (we may guess) a past instigator of it. Until his imprisonment he had what the prisoner could only dream about: a peaceful and secure family life. Like the vagrant, his predicament turns his thoughts immediately to his family and the aristocratic clan who include 'the chief of the army' and a liberal sprinkling of other 'Brothers / In the army and police' (p. 85). His immediate family must be protected from the knowledge of his humiliation: his wife must be told lies and his children and old mother must continue to receive money from him (pp. 84–8). The only suggestion that he has instigated violence is his confessed responsibility for 'Law and Order', but if we consider the violence and disorder of law in the poem that hint is enough. The assassin voice is associated with a love of violence, an enjoyment of the act itself, initially expressed in his delight in his own beautiful shooting and reinforced by the image of the *lek* lizard in the vagrant's cell, which

> Wields his deadly tongue
> And smashes a mosquito
> To death . . .
> There are tears of joy
> In his eyes! (p. 65).

Nevertheless he also has a family, a village clan, like that of the vagrant, and his imprisonment is destroying his relationship with them. He wants to return to the village for the 'cleansing ceremony', to protect himself from the 'vengeful ghost' of his victim, and to have his killing blessed by his mother and the clan elders (pp. 76–7) before he can claim the praise of the crowds he thinks want to celebrate the death of his victim. His love of family gives him none of the gentleness of the vagrant; every part of the three sections expresses the desire to celebrate the assassination and he even faces up to and accepts the way in which his action has destroyed his victim's family life. Section 9 extends the image of broken family relationships the three prisoners give us into a commonplace in the society through the young widow whose husband has been assassinated and then to all the victims of her husband's regime whose wives have only the memories of husbands to support them (pp. 72–3). The image of the black ants carrying away the dead termites and leaving only the 'queen mother / Of the hillock' behind again reinforces this picture.

'Song of Prisoner' describes a society in which men cannot fulfil their duties to their families because of the effects of poverty or political violence upon their family relationships. The impotence of the vagrant, like that of Ocol, represents the failure of men to hold their families together and ensure the continuation of the clan because their families are broken on the wheel of post-independence politics. The treacherous 'black Benz', the accepted symbol of arrival into the post-Independence élite because of all the new potency that goes with it, has torn through the grasses and shrubs and the anger of the village gods to prepare for the rape of the clan:

Big chief
Is dancing my wife
And cracking
My sacred rock. (p. 44)

The power of the 'spear that I trust' (see above, p. 54) has been replaced by the blunt invasion of the 'black Benz'. The poem's ending is one of despair for Okot's generation, despair for the immediate future. The desire to 'dance / And forget' helplessness before the certain destruction of the family implies an escape from reality, but the nationalities of the dancers keep the violence of the world in mind: 'Arabs' are close to 'Israelis', 'Russians' are paired with 'Germany'; 'Vietnamese', 'colonialists', 'communists' and 'ex-Nazis' all recall images of violent struggle. The vagrant cannot escape. In the final section of the poem he sings with the jazz musicians from the night club of the destruction in the wake of the conflagrations of violence that have engulfed many parts of Africa and mixed his 'bile' with theirs (p. 116) in a succession of bitter ironies. The Nigerian 'High life' tune is juxtaposed with the wailing of orphans; yams and human bones lie together in 'neat heaps' in the market place and the 'ash' of destroyed food, like manna, falls 'gently on the heads / Of starving children' (p. 114).

The prisoner's 'Song' differs from Lawino's both in the time it describes and the place: it concerns urban, not rural Africa. Okot sees no future for Ocol's 'New City' but this does not destroy his dream of the 'New Village'. Lawino told Ocol:

The ways of your ancestors
Are good,
Their customs are solid
And not hollow
They are not thin, not easily breakable
They cannot be blown away
By the winds
Because their roots reach deep into the soil. (p. 29)

They have not been 'blown away'. The whirlwind of Amin's violence has destroyed a good deal of the colonial and bourgeois superstructure in Ugandan society but it has largely halted the determined post-Independence attack on the clan way of life. It is likely that the resilience which enabled the clans to survive the depredations of the slave-raiders and their enemies and the seductive offerings of the missionaries will stand in good stead those Acoli who survive, despite their enormous recent losses of human resources. Lawino warned Ocol that his threat to the *okango* on the ancestral shrine was a threat to his own survival, not to that of the clan (p. 214), but Ocol still promised to 'uproot / Every sacred tree' (*Song of Ocol*, pp. 23–4), and now he, like the vagrant, is:

> A broken branch of a Tree
> Torn down by the whirlwind
> Of Uhuru.
> (*Two Songs*, p. 118)

Notes to Chapter 8

1. Conversation with Okot p'Bitek.
2. See also B. A. Ogot, 'Intellectual Smugglers in Africa', *East Africa Journal*, December 1971.
3. For 'The kite with the flame / In its anus' see *Religion of the Central Lvo*, pp. 126–8; for '*jok Omara*', p. 115; for '*jok Odude*' and '*jok Ayweya*', p. 116; for '*jok Rubanga*', pp. 116–19; for the sorcery of 'some jealous woman' and 'Death in a bundle', pp. 130–3.
4. It should be noted that Fanon and Okot are most immediately concerned with different situations in that Fanon was writing in an anti-colonial struggle in an area where land alienation had taken place, whereas Okot is most concerned with the post-colonial struggle for power in Uganda, and especially its effects on Acoliland, an area where there was no land alienation. This difference in circumstances does not, however, completely explain their differing points of view.

Bibliography

Atieno, Odhiambo. 'Two Songs, a Discussion, 1,' in *Standpoints on African Literature* (Nairobi: East African Literature Bureau, 1973).

Adimola, A. B. 'The Lamogi Rebellion, 1911–12' *Uganda Journal*, Vol. XVIII, No. 2 (September, 1954).

Anywar, Reuben S. 'The Life of Rwot Iburaim Awic' *Uganda Journal*, Vol. XII, No. 1 (March, 1948).

Barber, J. P. 'The Moving Frontier of British Imperialism in Northern Uganda' *Uganda Journal*, Vol. XXIX, No. 1 (March, 1965).

p'Bitek, Okot. *Africa's Cultural Revolution* (Nairobi: Macmillan Books for Africa, 1973).

——. *Religion of the Central Luo* (Nairobi: East African Literature Bureau, 1971).

——. *Song of Lawino* (Nairobi: East African Publishing House, 1966; Cleveland, Ohio: World-Meridian Books, 1969).

——. *Lak Tar* (Nairobi: East African Literature Bureau, 1953).

——. *Horn of My Love* (London: Heinemann Educational Books, 1974; New York: Humanities Press, 1974).

——. *Song of Ocol* (Nairobi: East Africa Publishing House, 1970).

——. *Two Songs* (Nairobi: East African Publishing House, 1971).

——. *Wer pa Lawino* (Nairobi: East African Publishing House, 1969).

——. *African Religions in Western Scholarship* (Nairobi: East African Literature Bureau, 1971; Totowa, N. J.: Rowman and Littlefield, 1972).

——. *Song of a Prisoner* (New York: The Third Press, Joseph Okpaku Publishing Co. Inc., 1971).

——. 'Reflect, Reject, Recreate' *East African Journal* (April, 1972).

——. *Oral Literature and Its Social Background Among the Acoli and Lang'o* (B. Litt. thesis, University of Oxford, 1964).

Booth, Wayne C. *The Rhetoric of Fiction* (Chicago: The University of Chicago Press, 1961).

p'Chong, Cliff Lubwa. *Vernacular Themes in Our Schools* (Unpublished paper presented to the Makerere Golden Jubilee Writers' Workshop, University of Nairobi, December, 1972).

Diamond, Stanley (ed.). *Culture in History* (New York: Columbia University Press, 1960).

Duerden, Dennis and Cosmo Pieterse (eds.). *African Writers Talking* (London: Heinemann Educational Books, 1972; New York: Africana Publishing Co., 1972).

Fanon, Frantz. *The Wretched of the Earth* (London: Penguin Books, 1967; New York: Grove Press, 1965).

Finnegan, Ruth. *Oral Literature in Africa* (Oxford: Clarendon Press, 1970).

Frye, Northrop. *Anatomy of Criticism: Four Essays* (Princeton: Princeton University Press, 1957).

Gathungu, Maina. 'Okot p'Bitek: Writer, Singer or Culturizer,' in *Standpoints on African Literature* (Nairobi: East African Literature Bureau, 1973).

Girling, J. K. *The Acholi of Uganda* (London: HMSO, 1960).

Gray, J. Milner. 'Acoli History 1860–1901, Part 1' *Uganda Journal*, Vol. XV, No. 2 (September, 1951).

——. 'Acoli History 1860–1901, Part 2' *Uganda Journal*, Vol. XVI, No. 1 (March, 1952).

——. 'Acoli History 1860–1901, Part 3' *Uganda Journal*, Vol. XVI, No. 2 (September, 1952).

Hodgart, Matthew. *Satire* (London: Weidenfeld and Nicolson, World University Library, 1969).

Jones, Eldred (ed.). *African Literature Today, No. 6, Poetry in Africa* (London: Heinemann Educational Books, 1973; New York: Africana Publishing Co., 1973).

Kibera, Leonard, *Voices in the Dark* (Nairobi: East African Publishing House, 1970).

Killam, G. D. (ed.). *African Writers on African Writing* (London: Heinemann Educational Books, 1973).

Leys, Colin. *Politicians and Policies, An essay on politics in Acoli, Uganda, 1962–65* (Nairobi: East African Publishing House, 1967).

lo Liyong, Taban. *Eating Chiefs* (London: Heinemann Educational Books, 1970).

——. *The Last Word* (Nairobi: East African Publishing House, 1969).

pa'Lukobo, Okumo. 'Review of *Wer pa Lawino*' in *Nanga*, Vol. II, No. 3 (National Teachers' College, Kyambogo, Uganda, May, 1970).

Mbiti, John. *African Religions and Philosophy* (London: Heinemann Educational Books, 1969).

Moore, Gerald. 'Grasslands Poetry, a review of *Song of Lawino*' in *Transition*, No. 21, Vol. 51 (Kampala, June/July, 1967).

Ngugi wa Thiong'o. *Homecoming* (London: Heinemann Educational Books, 1972).

Ntiru, R. C. 'Review of *Two Songs*' in *East Africa Journal* (May, 1971).

Ocheng, D. O. 'Land Tenure in Acoli' *Uganda Journal*, Vol. XIX, No. 1 (March, 1955)

Oculi, Okello, *Prostitute* (Nairobi: East African Publishing House, 1968).

Ogot, B. A. 'Intellectual Smugglers in Africa' *East Africa Journal* (December, 1971).

Ojuka, Aloo. 'Two Songs, a Discussion, 2,' in *Standpoints on African Literature* (Nairobi: East African Literature Bureau, 1973).

Pollard, Arthur. *Satire* (London: Methuen and Co. Ltd., The Critical Idiom 7, 1969).

Rigby, Peter. 'Review of *African Religions in Western Scholarship*' in *Mawazo* Vol. III, No. 1 (June, 1971).

Russell, J. K. *Men Without God*? (London: The Highway Press, 1966).

Serumaga, Robert, *Return to the Shadows* (London: Heinemann Educational Books, 1969).

Wanjala, Chris L. (ed.). *Standpoints on African Literature* (Nairobi: East African Literature Bureau, 1973).

Zimiru, Pio and Gurr, Andrew (eds.)., *Black Aesthetics, Papers from a Colloquium held at the University of Nairobi, June,* 1971 (Nairobi: East African Literature Bureau, 1973).

Index